TABLE OF CO

Doing it for George

It's a Big Bad World
Meets *It's A Wonderful Life*

by
Robert David

ISBN: 978-1-9999480-0-9

Design/Typesetting (Interior): Chris Moore www.fromprinttoebook.com

Extract taken from *It's A Wonderful Life*,
Final Shooting Script, 1946

The whistle of an approaching train is heard.

George:

Thar she blows.
You know what the three most exciting sounds
in the world are?

Uncle Billy:

Uh-huh. Breakfast is served,
lunch is served, dinner…

George:

No, no, no, no!
Anchor chains, plane motors and train whistles.

Dedicated to travellers and the people everywhere who are kind to them.

ONE

Crouch End:
North London's Bedford Falls

It's A Wonderful Life is one of Hollywood's best loved films. It's always shown at Christmas, but if you don't know the movie, it tells the story of George Bailey, played by James Stewart, living in a small town in upstate New York called Bedford Falls. There's nothing remarkable about George. He's an ordinary guy who grows up in an ordinary town, but he does so with one stirring ambition. You see George may lack opportunity, but he doesn't lack imagination. As he says to the young Mary Hatch in the opening reel, "I'm shaking the dust of this crummy little town off my feet, and I'm going to see the world."

But despite all George's best efforts, circumstances always conspire to keep him within the small town confines of Bedford Falls. He becomes the archetypal good guy and a pillar of the community who touches everyone else's lives and in small ways changes them all for the better. Oh yes, and he grows up to marry Mary Hatch. Now, given that the role of Mary was played by Donna Reed this should have been enough to keep any man happily at home. If I'd been George Bailey, I would have gladly burned my passport at the altar as part of the wedding ceremony.

As the story unfolds we see that George's plans of getting away are always frustrated at the final moment. Eventually, he accepts the inevitable and settles down to family life and his job running the Bailey Building and Loan, a mortgage company with a conscience that helps the poorer citizens of Bedford Falls own their own homes. It's a pretty much nickel and dime business which struggles to stay solvent and make George much of a living. What makes life harder is that Bedford Falls is run by the greedy Mr. Potter who as George puts it, "owns half the town and would like to own the other half."

Then suddenly 8,000 dollars accidentally goes missing from the Bailey Building and Loan accounts. Being the boss George is responsible for it, and with the bank examiner arriving to do the books it looks like George is destined for ruin and prison. In desperation George turns to the only person who can possibly help him, Potter, only to be called, "a miserable little clerk crawling in here on your hands and knees begging for help. No securities, no stocks, no bonds, nothing but a miserable little 500 dollars equity in a life insurance policy. You're worth more dead than alive."

George flees into the snowy, storm-filled night with Potter's last words echoing in his ears. There's a truss bridge at the edge of town and George decides to throw himself off it into the dark, swirling, life-sucking waters. The fateful night is Christmas Eve, and the celestial powers that be up-stairs decide to send down an angel (second class) called Clarence to show George the error of his ways. Just as George is about to leap to his doom, he hears a shout and a body plunges past him and splashes into the water below. Instinct takes over and George immediately dives in to rescue the would-be suicide, who is none other than Clarence, the angel (second class).

This action saves George's life but Clarence's mission has only just begun. He has to make George realise that committing suicide would have been throwing away God's greatest gift, but George is still in no mood to be convinced. At first Clarence fails to persuade George that he's throwing away the most precious gift of all and then he comes up with an idea. Actually, George comes up with it when he tells Clarence, "I suppose it would have been better if I'd never been born at all."

To which Clarence responds, "Wait a minute. That's an idea." It's actually the idea that drives the movie. In order to convince George that his life hasn't been a total failure and that, on the contrary, George has been of real value to many people, Clarence shows George what life in Bedford Falls would have been like had George never lived. And as it turns out it's not a pretty sight. Also, in the hands of the director, Frank Capra, this intriguing idea for a story became one of the great high concept movies of all times, and a feel-good classic.

I can't remember exactly the first time I saw *It's A Wonderful Life.* It would have been on TV when I was a young teenager and I just happened across it. I certainly wasn't looking for it, in fact I'd never even heard of the film. What I do remember is the huge impact it had on me. I've watched it every Christmas since, and it's as much a part of the festivities for me as carol concerts and roast turkey. Christmas simply wouldn't be Christmas without watching *It's A Wonderful Life.*

Many years later I ended up as a film-maker myself working in a community film school in Ethiopia. We made what we called behaviour change drama films. Basically, these films were stories with an agenda that got people to think about issues in new ways. The films addressed HIV/AIDS, harmful cultural practices and promoted education and better health. The aim of these films was to inspire people to change their lives for the better. It was pure Frank Capra, and my lifelong affection for *It's A Wonderful Life* played a major role in putting me on that particular road. But first I had another road to travel.

There's a scene in the beginning of the film when Clarence is being briefed on his mission by one of his heavenly bosses, Joseph, who gives the angel some background information. Over a shot of George Bailey as a young boy we hear:

Joseph: That's him (George) when he was 12 back in 1919.

That means George Bailey was born in 1907. And given that the film was screened in 1947 that made George 40 years old when he had his mid-life crisis, which, according to the lifestyle magazines, would have been about par for the course. So being the singularly unimaginative chap that I am, when I turned 40 I had a little wobbly mid-life crisis moment of my own. I had spent the last 20 odd years working in advertising writing TV commercials. It had been fun. As a copywriter in a London ad agency I had fought my way to the top in various creative department shoot-outs. Briefly, I was that man, the fastest pun in the West. Well, West End anyway. But like all pun-slingers in the ad business, one day you're going to come up against someone out there who's going to be that split-second faster, and better, than you. And so it was. My High Noon moment came when a young creative team comprising two drop dead gorgeous looking young women were put on the account. Trouble was they had the brains, wit and creativity to go with it too. And no little style. Anyway, I reasoned to myself, after ten years my work had got a bit samey. The truth was, of course, that it wasn't the work at all. It was me that had got a lot samey, and when the clients started to recognise another batch of my second-hand reworked ideas, I knew my number was up. In the finest traditions of the business the agency got its retaliation in first and I was paid off. So there I was, jobless on the one hand and completely clueless on the other about what to do with my life. I was too old for the business but too young to retire. I was also wife-less and kid-less. Like a lot of people in this predicament I attacked the problem by watching lots of daytime television. It was the run-up to Christmas and while all my ex-colleagues were quaffing champagne at various client Christmas parties around town, I was busy lounging it on the sofa. Being Christmas, *It's A Wonderful Life* came on and as per usual I watched it again. As I witnessed for the umpteenth time George's familiar struggle with himself a vague notion began to take shape in my mind. But the idea really hit me in the scene where George is talking to Uncle Billy at the train station. They're there to meet George's brother, Harry Bailey, a returning war hero.

The whistle of an approaching train is heard.

George: Thar she blows. You know what the three most exciting sounds in the world are?

Uncle Billy: Uh-huh. Breakfast is served, lunch is served, dinner...

George: No, no, no, no! Anchor chains, plane motors and train whistles.

George's passion to go out and see something of the world had always touched me, but before I had never given that part of the story more than a passing thought. Wait a minute, I realised, perhaps I don't have to go straight back in and find another job, I could go travelling. After all, travelling was supposed to be good for the soul, so I began to wonder what it might do for my muddled mind. The more I thought about it the more I realised that unlike George I didn't have a Mary Bailey to keep me at home, and Mary aside, the only reason George never realised his dream and went travelling was because he simply never got the chance. Now here I was with that chance on a plate.

I may not have shared George's driving passion for seeing the world but travel had always lingered in the back of my mind. I had just never got round to it. Too many things had always got in the way though: getting a degree, finding a job, clawing one's way onto the property ladder, scheming for that next promotion, re-mortgaging to pay for the kitchen extension, that sort of stuff. The gap year thing had passed me by too. Back then if you'd have asked me was I "taking off" after university, it would have meant had I secured a ground-floor position with a thrusting multinational, and hopefully with a maroon Mondeo thrown in. No, to date my travelling experiences had been taken from the pages of Thomas Cook brochures, not the Lonely Planet. The one possible exception was during my student days when my girlfriend Sharon and I went to Paris for a long weekend. We were both 19 and were desperately in love the way only teenagers can be. Paris did not disappoint and lived up to every romantic expectation, even if we couldn't do it in the style the city deserved. But, just strolling the streets of Montmartre hand-in-hand; killing time in cafes talking about Jean Paul Sartre in very loud voices; torturing waiters with my schoolboy French; and finding cheap restaurants to eat in every evening was a complete adventure. At Charles de Gaulle airport on the way home I realised I no longer had my airline ticket. With minutes to go, there we were in the middle of the concourse: suitcases open, dirty shirts, socks and knickers being tossed into the air as we desperately searched for it. Then I had what I thought was a brainwave. The idea was for Sharon to fly back on the remaining ticket and with the remaining 14 francs we had left between us, I would hitchhike all the way back to Leicester, where we were at university. I thought it would be a great adventure. Sharon thought I was barking. In the end we found the offending ticket with seconds to spare and sprinted for the check-in. My big chance to do some intrepid travelling had been snatched away from me, and we had just experienced our first serious lovers' row – thanks Paris. To this day I still haven't been back there.

A couple of weeks later it was New Year's Eve and I found myself in the Harringay Arms in Crouch End with my two good friends Tricia and Cathy. Tricia was Australian but had lived in London for years and Cathy, being younger than me, had done the travelling thing and had lived and worked in Australia years before. Every few years or so Tricia went back to visit friends and family. Without warning Tricia looked up and said, "You know I'm going back to Australia for next New Year's, don't you?" which I did. "Well," she continued, "why don't you come out too?"

"Sure," I slurred, "great idea."

"No, I'm serious," she said, "think about it, what's stopping you?"

She had a point. I mulled the idea over for a few days and it began to take on a more definite shape. Then the thought hit me. If I was going to go halfway round the world, what was the point of coming back the same way, why not simply continue going on round? That way I could do the hippy backpacker destinations like India and Thailand on the way out, and the road trip USA thing on the way back. Then another thought hit me: if I was going to be in America perhaps there was a Bedford Falls

I could visit. I started researching the idea and came across a town in upstate New York that called itself the Real Bedford Falls. According to its website, Seneca Falls is convinced it's the inspiration for the fictional town in the film. Capra visited Seneca Falls before he made the film and heard the true story about a man who threw himself into the river to save a suicide, like Clarence does for George in the movie. But what really sealed it was that Karolyn Grimes, who played George's daughter, Zuzu, in the movie was a regular visitor when they held their annual *It's A Wonderful Life* weekends. She was also the last surviving member of the cast and I figured if Seneca Fall's claim to be the real Bedford Falls was good enough for Zuzu Bailey, it was good enough for me. I decided to make it the culmination of my trip, and I also made myself a promise that if I made it round the world and got to Seneca Falls, I was going to meet her.

Now that I had an aiming point, I bought a round-the-world airline ticket and started planning my trip: India, Thailand, Singapore, Hong Kong, Australia and the USA. I had no idea what George would have thought of my itinerary. My guess is he would have loved it. George, I reckoned, had the heart and soul of a true traveller. He knew that it didn't matter so much where you went, it's how you get there that matters and who you meet along the way, and if you're really lucky you may just learn a little bit more about yourself as well as the people and places you pass through. So there I was, a mature man, experienced in business and the ways of the world, and that world had somehow, miraculously just become my oyster. What could possibly go wrong? If George had ever found himself in my position, I reckoned, he'd have been off like a shot. So, as payback for all those Christmas reruns I had enjoyed so much, I thought that going travelling was the very least I could do for the old boy. I would do it in his honour. I would do it for George.

TWO
Rail Raj

I emerged blinking into India, that is if it's possible to blink while your eyes are out on stalks. The cliché has it that India assaults all the senses and it's true. Actually it mugs them, and all at once. I emerged from the airport concourse to be struck by a barrage of blinding sunlight, heat, hordes of people which included rickshaw wallahs, taxi drivers, fellow passengers, beggars, street urchins and noise. I didn't have time to take it all in as I was a man on a mission. I only had a couple of hours to get to New Delhi station and pick up my Indrail ticket reservations which I had booked a few weeks earlier in the UK. While planning the India leg of my journey I had been inspired by an idea by Gandhi. As a young man he once asked a senior figure how he should get to know India. He was told to see it from the window of a train, and I thought if that was good enough advice for the Mahatma, it was certainly good enough for me.

I had bought my Indrail pass in the UK's only India Rail ticket agency in Wembley. The agency was run by Dr. Dandapani, officially the world's greatest living expert on India's colossal and diverse railway system, and unofficially India's charm ambassador to Britain. He had been extremely helpful planning the India leg of my journey, and could quote the names of express trains and their departure and arrival times out of thin air. It had been a very impressive performance, and I got the distinct impression that the good doctor actually having to consult a timetable would have been akin to Olivier calling for the prompt halfway through Hamlet's soliloquy. My rail pass entitled me to go anywhere I wanted on the entire subcontinent's railway system. Although the distances between places in India can be vast, flying is simply far too expensive for most Indians, and going by road is not as quick as going by rail. Consequently, most people travel by train, and in a country made up of a thousand million people, the term "everyone" means a hell of a lot of people. This means, or so the good doctor explained, that there is always a far greater demand for rail tickets than there are places on trains. This made having confirmed reservations on trains an absolute necessity, which meant planning my travelling in India, and booking my train tickets, in advance.

I had opted to start my train travelling at Agra, home of the Taj Mahal, and from there go to Lucknow, one of the scenes of the bloody Indian Mutiny. From there I planned to train it to Varanasi, the spiritual heart of Hindu India and the home of the ghats, the steps that lead down to the bathing places in the sacred River Ganges. Next stop would be Darjeeling for a little old-style Raj relic hill station charm. Calcutta would come next being by way of a total contrast being one of India's most frenetic metropolises, and then finally back to Delhi.

I struggled through the throng towards the taxi rank and was immediately besieged by a horde of taxi drivers competing for my fare. "Beautiful taxi, very safe," shouted one driver above the general din, and recognising a well communicated consumer benefit when I heard one, I gave him the nod. But still the throng of other taxi drivers wasn't giving up on the prospect of a fare, and hands reached out and tugged at me as my driver forced a pathway through the crowd to the kerbside, before unceremoniously bundling me into the back of a small car and throwing my backpack on top of me. By the time I had righted myself he had slipped in behind the wheel and gunned the engine.

"And where is it you will be going?" he asked.

"Dehli station," I replied.

"And how are you liking very much my Ambassador?" he asked, as without apparent regard for the tsunami of rickshaws, tuk tuks and other vehicles that streamed past my window, he let out the clutch and lurched into the river of traffic. Miraculously, we joined it without any tearing screeches of metal on metal. It took me a moment to realise he was talking about the taxi. "Hindustan Ambassador is very good car," he went on, "we are making it here in India like your Morris Oxford of Great Britain." It was obvious that he was inordinately proud of his car, and the fact that he had a member of the mother country slumped on its back seat made him feel all the prouder for it. "Very nice," I said. And it certainly had a charm all of its own. It was small and I guessed that three people in the back would have been a very tight squeeze indeed. So first impressions suggested it was more of a "second secretary for consular affairs" than a full blown ambassador. But that said it was fun. Its engine chugged in a friendly kind of way, the upholstery was smooth and well worn, and it bobbed along the pitted road with a bouncy gait. If Noddy had driven a limo, this would have been it. It was baking hot inside the little taxi and I noticed that the window by my side had a wind-me down handle attached to the door. It took a good six revolutions for the window to lower itself about half an inch. So it took me well over a minute of constant winding to lower the window halfway down. By this time the car was filled by a cloud of smoke exhaust and general fug that had my eyes streaming, so it took me another minute, coughing and spluttering, to wind the window up again.

When Delhi station hove into view I thought he had taken me somewhere else by mistake. The last time I had seen such a spectacular looking imperial edifice was when I had been taken as a kid to see the Tutankhamen exhibition at the British Museum. It turned out to be a station all right, only trouble was it was the wrong one. A very charming elderly man at the ticket office informed me that this was Delhi station, but I needed New Delhi station.

"Not to be worrying," he said, as he took me by the arm and led me over to a crowded platform, "if you are taking the next train from this platform," he said, "New Delhi station is two stops down the line."

A few minutes later a train pulled up at the platform and I hoisted myself aboard. The carriage was separated into standing and seating sections. The seats were bare wooden benches. It was crowded with workers and school children returning home to the suburbs. Late afternoon sunshine dazzled through the glassless windows and doors. The men sat in groups, talking and laughing loudly. To my left a group of half a dozen men were sitting cross-legged around a mound of naan bread and a bowl of dahl, a thin looking lentil soup. Every so often they would peel off strips of the naan bread, dunk it in the grey-green dahl, tilt their heads back and drop it into their mouths. All the seats were occupied by men while the women passengers hunkered down on the dusty floor, which from time to time was routinely swept by any one of a small army of children with makeshift brooms made of palm fronds. It seemed to be their job to wage an un-winnable war against the waves of dust and dirt that filtered in through the open windows and doors. Not to mention from the thousands of bare feet, sandals and the occasional pair of shoes that entered the carriages. The women were all dressed the same, poorly, and they contented themselves with chewing on beetle nuts, which they popped into the bright orange cavities of their toothless mouths with open-palmed hands which made popping noises. In stark contrast, schoolboys from middle class, well-to-do Indian families stood stiffly to attention in their starched white shirts, bright red school ties, knee-high socks and black shiny shoes which matched perfectly the sheen of their slicked back neatly combed hair. They, like everyone else, totally ignored the urchin sweeper-wallahs as they scurried around their feet conjuring up little dust devils with flicks of their wrists. The schoolboys, like everybody else, were far too busy staring at me.

New Delhi station looked much like its older namesake. Now I had done my fair share of commuting into the mainline London stations during the rush hour, but nothing had prepared me for New Delhi station in full human flood on a weekday evening. The platforms, and there must have been over 20 of them, thronged not just with ordinary passengers, but also with hordes of beggars with hands outstretched and sightless eyes shuffling along in bare feet and dressed in rags; soldiers in almost-but-not-quite matching uniforms in transit; policemen looking more military than the soldiers in their perfect khaki uniforms and long wooden canes topped with brass knobs; rich women in silk saris, food hawkers pushing trolleys piled high with pastries, fresh fruit and gaudily coloured sweets; and the ever present *chai* wallahs passing tin cups of tea through the bars of the windows of the carriages to thirsty passengers. Just when I thought I had seen it all, a cow ambled down the platform without a care in the world.

I fought my way through the crowds looking for a sign that would direct me to the reservations office. When I eventually found one it pointed me up an ornate marble staircase that wouldn't have looked out of place in the grand home of a Hapsburg count. Inside, the booking office was very busy. Half a dozen booking clerks bustled about with sheaves of papers and tickets in their hands. They were being despatched hither and thither by a middle aged man who occupied the seat of power in the office. How could I tell? It was the only one. Oh, and he was also the only one wearing a tie. He sat at a large desk in the middle of the room that overflowed with papers. Passengers and bookings clerks alike waited on his every word and gesture. I joined a queue of about 20 Indian passengers but being the only European I was promptly called over by one of the minions. If the others who had been waiting a great deal longer than me minded, they had the courtesy not to let it show. In fact, I was greeted by shy smiles and greetings of *namaste*, which were accompanied by hands being placed together as if in prayer and little bows of the head.

I handed over the documents, which had looked very official in Wembley, but not so impressive now. The clerk took them, studied them for a bit, hauled down and leafed through a couple of over-stuffed lever-arch files, and scratched his head a lot. He came up empty. Obviously there was nothing else for it, this was a job for *the man*. He marched over to the man at the table and presented my documents to him and pointed at me. I smiled nervously. Anyway it seemed to do the trick. The great man ceased from despatching acolytes left and right, hushed the crowd of gabbling Indian passengers before him with a scowl, pulled down his half moon glasses from the crown of his glistening pate, and gave my scraps of paper his total and undivided attention. My bookings clerk bent low to catch the whispered words of wisdom. Finally, the great man scrawled his initials on the bottom of my document, stuffed the papers back into the clerk's hands, and with a curt word and a nod sent him off in the direction of one of the few battered and worn out looking computer terminals that whirred and chugged in a corner of the office. The bookings clerk did the necessary key-punching and a couple of minutes later a printer choked, rather than spat out, a sheaf of printed tickets on perforated paper, each one detailing the name of my train, the station of departure, the number of the sleeper car and the number of the berth inside it. But first I had to get to Agra, and thinking that I would be seeing a lot of the inside of trains, I thought I'd take the bus for a change. Big mistake.

The number of people who die each year on India's roads must be staggeringly high. One of the problems is that they seem to have taken their caste system and applied it to whatever they have which passes for a highway code. There seemed to be a pecking order for all road users, just as there is for people in all other walks of Indian life. The untouchables were the pedestrians. It was open season on them. Cars and lorries didn't even bother to swerve to avoid pedestrians. If someone got hit and splattered all over the road it was their lookout. This tended to make pedestrians in India understandably fleet of foot when crossing the road. The road between Delhi and Agra is one of the busiest in the entire country. Next day, as we set out in the peaceful, early morning, there was no hint of what lay in store. However, as we left the outskirts of the city behind us things began to hot up.

For one of the country's major arteries it soon became remarkably undeveloped. For a start it was only two lanes wide, and when I say that

I don't mean two lanes going one way and two the other. All the traffic, north and south, had one lane each, which made overtaking a bit of an adventure and not for the faint-hearted. There wasn't even a white line down the middle of the road to differentiate one lane from the other. Not that anyone would have paid much attention if there had been. The term "road" also proved to be somewhat misleading. For most of us the word conjures up a picture of a smooth tarmac surface wide enough for approaching vehicles to pass in opposite directions without hitting each other. If this picture matches your vision too, think again. Quite often the tarmac gave way to long stretches of sun baked earth, or stretches of mud ground flat by the wheels of countless vehicles. When the tarmac did reassert itself, quite often it was dotted with pot-holes that were deep enough to rip off the axle of an armoured personnel vehicle. There was no kerb to speak of, just a jagged edge that was steadily being eroded by the encroaching countryside. Heading in each direction were buses jam-packed with people, but which seemed to have more paying passengers hanging off the sides than were actually inside them; brightly painted lorries decked out in tinsel which were piled so high with assorted goods that they swayed alarmingly with every tug on the steering wheel and threatened to topple over at any moment. Plus there were cars, vans, motorbikes and every kind of rickshaw that included bicycle rick-shaws, tricycle rickshaws and auto rickshaws. It wasn't uncommon to see the occasional motor scooter carrying an entire family consisting of Mum and Dad, Grannie and three or four of the kids. There were cyclists too. And carts pulled by buffaloes and camels. Every vehicle zigzagged through the traffic without any seeming regard as to what was coming the other way or who was overtaking from behind. If this wasn't mayhem enough, things turned really ugly every time a cow wondered onto the road, which was often. Cows being sacred this tended to create the emergency stop from hell as bare brown feet jumped on brake pedals and the din of hundreds of rusting brake discs, screeching against their equally ferrous wheel hubs, was enough to set teeth on edge in neighbouring states.

Not that the cows ever seemed overly concerned. Their normal practice was to view the surrounding bedlam they had just caused with total indifference, lift their tails, urinate, and saunter off. So it's small wonder that the humble pedestrian ever gets a look in. Given the choice between pranging a Brahman cow or a lowly caste father of six, not many Indian road users would think twice before jerking the steering wheel in the direction of the beast of burden on two legs.

I viewed all this from my ringside seat at the front of the bus right behind the driver. As soon as he got out on the open road he pushed the accelerator pedal to the floor and kept it there — no matter what. As the bus crept up on each slower moving vehicle, the driver would lean on the horn and simply pull out into the opposing stream of traffic in order to overtake, no matter what was coming the other way. I managed to endure half an hour of seeing him play chicken with every bus and lorry heading towards Delhi before I had to admit my nerves were shot. I retreated to the rear of the bus and tucked myself into the corner of the bench seat that stretched across the back. I had just about got my heart rate back to something approaching normal when I made the mistake of glancing out through the rear window. There, entirely filling my field of vision, was a huge lorry. It too was going at full throttle and unlike our driver did not seem remotely interested in taking any overtaking action whatsoever. It just kept coming at us; blaring its horn and no doubt expecting us to deftly sidestep out of its way. I am no mechanic, but even I could tell at a glance that this vehicle had been made up of so many spare parts. The headlamps were missing, the radiator grill looked like it had come from a combine harvester, the ill-fitting bumpers were held on by twists of wire, and there was no tax disc in the windscreen, simply because there was no windscreen. So whether or not it possessed a working set of brakes was anyone's guess. Somehow it managed to squeeze past us without leaving a layer of its rusting paintjob smeared all down one side. Once was enough, but overtaking encounters like this occurred about once every five minutes, and it took five hours to get to Agra.

Everyone goes to Agra to see the Taj Mahal, and I was no exception. The best time to see the Taj is at dawn and next morning I was up at 6.00am and took a rickshaw down there. In the soft, buttery early morning Indian light the Taj seemed to shimmer, light as a butterfly, on a sea of polished marble. It was too early for the crowds and school parties and I had the place virtually to myself. There were only a few other early riser visitors quietly wandering around. Each of us was lost in our own quiet reverie.

My Lonely Planet guide book told me that it was built by the Mughal Emperor, Shah Jahan, as a mausoleum for his wife, Mumtaz Mahal. She was his second wife and died during childbirth in 1631. She was his favourite, and legend has it that the Shah was so distraught at the news of her death that his hair turned grey overnight. Either that or the road to Delhi was just as bad in his day. The Taj is also one of the Seven Wonders of the World. Not bad for what ranks as a temporal pipsqueak, given that it stands alongside the pyramids. But for most people the Taj is the world's most famous monument to eternal love. Or at least it was until Princess Diana pitched up and famously posed for a photo *sans* Charles as it were. Up until that moment, the Taj had reigned supreme as the most romantic place in the world. But as a result of Diana looking all misty-eyed and lonesome gazing into the lenses of the world's press, overnight the Taj was promptly relegated to a position only a couple of notches above Chernobyl. What Diana's PR posturing had done to put a dent in the Indian tourist industry long term, I couldn't tell. But judging by the couples queuing up to have their photos taken on the "Diana bench" it looked like the Taj's place in the hearts and minds of lovers everywhere was assured. By mid morning the place was packed, although probably not by Indian standards. But 10,000 people crammed into a space about the size of half a dozen football pitches I found distinctly cosy, especially when the heat bouncing off the acres of white marble was enough to dry eyeballs. All that said, considering I had grown up seeing the Taj's image on a hundred biscuit tins and tea towels, and not forgetting the thousands of calendars in a hundred Indian take-aways, it truly was a magnificent sight.

I wondered what George would have thought of the Taj. George, after all, was something of a builder. He could also be a true romantic. Early in the movie George is at his brother Harry's graduation dance party at the local high school gym, when Mary Hatch's brother asks George to dance with his kid sister. Earlier in the film we had seen a six years old Mary confess that she was going to love George Bailey till the day she dies, but George, with his dreams of travelling the world, never showed any interest. George is reluctant at first and tries to make excuses. Then the crowd parts and George sees Mary as a young woman for the first time. It's a classic reveal, giving the female lead her first signature shot in the movie. George looks and the camera cuts to his point of view as he sees Mary as if for the first time, and the audience also sees Donna Reed for the first time in mid close up as Mary. One of the attributes that makes a Hollywood star is their ability to take the intense scrutiny of a close up and still look ravishing. Admittedly, there are a few tricks of the trade that can help, like the attentions of the hair and make-up departments, soft back lighting, and a 30 denier silk stocking stretched over the lens, but the basic raw material has to be there in the first place. And boy did Donna Reed have it. Even so, playing Mary Hatch was a very challenging role for the 25 years old, relatively unknown actress from Iowa to pull off. She had to be a looker, but she also had to exude a small-town homeliness. I don't know if the casting brief still exists for the role of Mary, but it would probably say something along the lines of… Mary is a young woman, likeable and popular, a very pretty girl who wins enough attention to know it but who wears it lightly. She has looks that turn heads, but it never goes to hers. If that wasn't a tough enough call on its own, the young Donna Read also had to contend with holding her own playing scenes with one of Hollywood's biggest stars and most popular leading men in Jimmy Stewart.

It's obvious that Mary knows that she and George are made for each other. In fact, the whole town knows it, everyone that is except George. They start to dance.

George: Well, hello.

Mary: Hello. You look at me as if you didn't know me.

George: Well, I don't.

Mary: You've passed me on the street almost every day.

George: Me?

Mary: Uh-huh.

George: Uh-huh. That was a little girl named Mary Hatch. That wasn't you.

George and Mary's path of true love runs relatively smoothly in the early part of the film and inevitably they get married. Even so this doesn't appear to have dampened George's wanderlust. As we see when Ernie the taxi driver is taking them to the train station on the start of their honeymoon. George has been saving up for this and he hands Mary a bunch of money.

George: You know what we're going to do. We're going to shoot the works. A whole week in New York. A whole week in Bermuda. The highest hotels – the oldest champagne – the richest caviar – the hottest music, and the prettiest wife.

Of course, circumstances conspire once again to make sure George never leaves Bedford Falls even on his honeymoon. There's a run on the banks and George has to give up his honeymoon to save the Bailey Building & Loan. But there's no doubting the old boy had style and given the chance I'm damn sure George would have whisked Mary off to the Taj Mahal like a shot.

I didn't have a Mary to keep me lingering any longer at the Taj, so I set off to see what else Agra had to offer apart from Mughal monuments. As I emerged from the Taj I was surrounded by a gaggle of competing cycle rickshaw wallahs. "Where you go, Sir", "Rickshaw very quick-quick", "Am being safest rickshaw in Agra".

"No thank you," I shouted in a loud voice, and preferring to walk, I headed off along the dusty street. I had not gone more than 20 yards before, and with a ping of his bicycle bell, one of the rickshaws appeared beside me. They all looked the same, large adult sized tricycles with bench seats at the back. It was "driven" by a wiry, young man dressed in a t-shirt and what appeared to be a grubby table cloth wrapped round his waist, which extended to mid calf. On his feet he wore cheap plastic flip-flops that had obviously seen better days.

"Where you going, Sir? Me take you," he said, standing upright on the pedals as he slowly kept pace with me.

"I'm just going for a walk, thank you," I replied.

"But it is being very hot, Sir, good rickshaw, good price."

"No thank you, I like to walk." I quickened my pace, but it didn't shake him off.

"But road is being very dangerous, not good Sir."

"No thank you," I said more firmly and quickened my pace again so that I was now almost jogging. He didn't have to break sweat to keep up with me though.

"I am knowing very good places to go, I have a cousin who…"

"Look, I don't want to take a rickshaw I want to walk, okay." By now I was getting exasperated. I stopped dead in my tracks and glared at him. He seemed to get the message and with a small smile and shrug of his shoulders he wheeled about and headed back the way he had come. I continued my walk and a few seconds later another ping of a bicycle bell announced the presence of another rickshaw.

"Hello Sir, it is being very beautiful day, where are you going?" It was another rickshaw wallah. I turned round only to see that half a dozen of them were lined up, one after the other, and had been slowly following me from the moment I left the Taj. They were simply going to take it in turns to try and get my fare. It took me a couple of minutes arguing to despatch this one, and as soon as he left "ding-ding" another one popped up in his place. Then I had an idea. There was no pavement to speak of and I had been walking in the same direction as the traffic so it had been relatively easy for them to hold station behind me like a convoy of naval frigates following a battleship. I crossed over the road so that now I was walking against the oncoming traffic, making it a great deal more difficult for them to keep shadowing me, or so I thought. To a man they all rose to the challenge, and with much blaring of horns and screeching of brakes from the passing traffic, they all followed me across the road blindly like little ducks waddling after their mother. They fanned out behind me, ringing their bells and jostling for position, oblivious to the oncoming buses, lorries and cars that hooted and swerved around them. There was no shaking them off, and my conscience was beginning to tell me that if I didn't hop into one of them soon, there was going to be a fatality. So I flagged one down and told him to take me to the Taj Ganz area of town.

My grateful rickshaw wallah dropped me off at the edge of the maze of narrow streets and alleyways. I ventured in. I found myself standing in a narrow street of small mud brick houses, which was crowded with people. An old man wearing only a grubby *dhoti* wrapped round his loins hurried past me herding a flock of scrawny goats. As I picked my way around the potholes and an open sewer that ran down the middle of the street, I had to dodge large carts piled high with vegetables and fruit, which creaked and groaned under the weight they carried, and were pulled by pairs of water buffaloes, their horns curled like corkscrews and their noses dribbling constantly like schoolboys with colds. Other carts were drawn by camels which looked strangely out of place prowling the city streets. At intervals, buses and lorries would announce themselves with teeth-rattling blasts of their horns as they roared past me with inches to spare. They rocked ridiculously from side to side on what passed for their suspensions as they negotiated the potholes, looking like ungainly tankers in a storm tossed sea. I passed women, many of whom carried heavy, earthenware pots or brass water jars on their heads, or stacks of sun-dried firewood. They may have been barefoot, dressed in dusty saris and had a couple of children hanging off their hips, but each one of them was possessed of the most striking elegance. They moved with swan-like grace and a sinuous poise that would have been the envy of many a cat-walk model. By the roadsides old women hunkered down on their haunches and patted out dung bricks with repeated slaps of their bare hands. There were no pavements so the shops, houses and workshops opened right on to the street and the passing traffic, which meant that everyone had to shout to be heard. Every shop seemed to have a radio or television with the volume cranked up to the highest level. People hurled greetings across the street at each other, and insults as well as far as I could make out. A tractor roared into life spewing thick, black, clogging clouds of carbon monoxide into my face. Every other business seemed to be an auto repair shop of some description. The air was ripped with the constant cacophony of hundreds of hammers banging on un-yielding metal. Babies wailed and angry mothers scolded naughty kids. Street life, I realised, was all noise, heat, noise, smell, noise, sweat, and more noise. Everything happened in the street: rotis were baked, tools sharpened, chins shaved, machines fixed, goats butchered, children taught, deals done, tempers lost, clothes washed and bowels opened. Pigs buried their snouts into piles of foul smelling rubbish. Cows wandered wherever they wanted, their trails marked by wet patches of rank smelling urine that dried quickly in the hot sun. Cats and dogs snoozed in patches of shade oblivious to the potentially decapitating wheels of the carts and buses that brushed past their noses. At the sight of me, naked children would bolt from their mothers, laps and run up to me shouting "*Allo, Allo*" or "*Ram-Ram*" or "*Namaste*" in greeting. As walks on the wild side go it was bedlam, and it was brilliant.

The first leg of my train travelling was aboard the exotically named Avadh Express, which departed from Agra Fort station at 21.55 and arrived at Lucknow at 06.30 the following morning. The station was only a few miles from my hotel and I gave myself plenty of time to get there by leaving the hotel with an hour to spare, or so I thought. When I emerged into the night through the gates of the hotel, there was, for once, not a single rickshaw wallah to be seen. This was strange because during the day every time I stepped outside the hotel the scene resembled India's annual rickshaw wallahs' convention. I stood around for a couple of minutes and then one materialised out of the gloom.

"Agra station," I told him in that slow, deliberate, talking to a child way I had embarrassingly seemed to have adopted. "How much?"

"That is being 50 rupees," he said, staring me straight in the eye with a sense of challenge. The gall of the man. Earlier, when the place was swarming with rickshaws and some of the old free market competition laws of competition were at work, the fare would have been ten rupees, tops. I decided to go along with the game and enter into a bit of bargaining. It would be rude not to.

"20 rupees, " I said, hoisting my backpack up ready to throw it on the seat as the deal was sure to be done.

"Begging pardon Sir, no, the fare is being 50 rupees," he said with all the confidence of a solitary rickshaw wallah talking to a tourist in a hurry not to miss his train standing on a lonely corner in Agra in the middle of the night. Thump went the backpack as I dropped it on the ground.

"30 rupees," I said, adding, "and that's my final offer." Surely no rickshaw-wallah in his right mind was going to pass up on 30 rupees. It was well over three times as much as he would normally get and the chances of another passenger happening along at this time of night were pretty slim. My offer of 30 rupees had to represent a real bonus at the end of a hard working day, one he would be sure to boast about when he got home to the wife.

"No, Sir, the fare is still being 50 rupees," he said. "50 rupees to Agra station is being very good price."

He wasn't budging. He was sticking to his guns and holding out for the full 50 rupees. Pride got the better of me and I picked up my backpack again and strode off into the dark in indignation. In ten minutes not a single rickshaw had passed me. Twenty minutes later I was stood at the side of a dark backstreet, with no idea of where I was and beginning to panic. Then a doddery old fellah huffing and puffing on a cycle rickshaw happened along. He must have been seventy if he was a day. But he scooped the jackpot because I did not dare to argue with him over the price, which he struck at 30 rupees. I hopped in but it only took me a couple of minutes to realise that my problems might not be over. As well as being of a venerable age, he was also very thin and if he had weighed in at more than six stone I would have been very surprised. I've seen more muscle on a string bean. The prospect of pedalling a thirteen stone man, complete with bulging backpack, across five miles of unkempt roads, could prove all together too much for his skeletal frame, I thought. Anyway, we set off. I'm afraid I have to admit that the situation rather brought out the worst in me. I completely failed to appreciate that in all likelihood he was completely exhausted after a hard day hauling similarly overweight tourists up and down to the Taj. Every time he momentarily rested on his pedals, or as he took a deep breath to brace himself before an incline, I whipped him back into action, barking "Chaldi! Chaldi!" at him. To give him his due though, he struggled manfully through the pitch-dark streets with the passenger from hell and still managed to get me to the station in time. I paid him off, trying to assuage my conscience at the same time with a hefty tip. He helped me on with my backpack and gently pushed me in the direction of the regal looking archway that marked the entrance to the station, no doubt glad to see the back of me.

Inside the station concourse it was gloomy. A single bare bulb struggled to illuminate the large vestibule that housed the ticket office. I went through and straight on to the platform, which was crowded with passengers: lone travellers, couples and entire extended families who occupied every available square inch of platform. Armed guards in smart uniforms patrolled up and down looking for all the world like self-important toy soldiers. Food wallahs pushed little carts through the crowd selling sweets, pastries and bottled drinks. I stopped one and bought a couple of packets of dry biscuits and a litre of mineral water, hard tack for the journey ahead. A glance to my right told me that the platform was lined with offices. Each office door was topped with a hand-painted sign and one of them was too good to be true: the Assistant Vigilance Officer. I poked my head round the door. The space was large and airy with a very high ceiling. A naked bulb threw a pale glow into the gloom. Three men who didn't look particularly vigilant, it has to be said, sat around a bare desk idly leafing through piles of paperwork. Hopefully not complaints, I thought. One of them looked up as I crashed through their doorway under the weight of my backpack.

"Excuse me," I said. "I have reservation on a second class sleeper carriage on the Avadh Express, and I've never travelled on a train in India before…"

I left the sentence sort of hanging in the air, a bit like conversational ground bait, in the hope that one of them would pick up on it. The one who had looked up as I entered reached out his hand and asked, "May I please be looking at your ticket?" I dug around in the side pocket of my backpack and proffered the necessary.

"The process is being very simple," he said peering at me over the half moon spectacles that had appeared from his top pocket and which gave him the air of a rather bored and patient primary school teacher dealing with a particularly dim child. "There are being three second class sleeper carriages on this train. When it is arriving in the station the conductor will be posting a list of the names of passengers with tickets by the door of each carriage. If you are having a reservation your name is being on the list."

"Oh, right," I said. "So all I have to do is look for my name on the list that's stuck up on the carriage."

"And when you are finding your name there is being a number next to it. This number is being the number of your berth where you are sleeping." And with that he returned my rail pass. He was right, I thought, what could be simpler.

"The second class sleepers are being near the middle of the train," he said by way of an afterthought. "If you are standing on the platform outside this office, you will be nearing the right place when the train is coming."

I thanked him for this extra nugget of information and left, reflecting it was actually very vigilant of him to have told me that. Outside there wasn't a spare patch of platform to be seen. It was completely covered in people and their luggage. They either sat or lay fully stretched out on the concrete floor of the platform seemingly oblivious to the crush of humanity all around them. It was so crowded that even the monkeys that normally scampered up and down the platforms had been driven onto the rails. They sat in bored groups picking fleas from one another, only stirring themselves when someone dropped a crust or piece of fruit peel.

The Avadh Express announced its arrival with a low, mournful whistle. As one the passengers rose to their feet like a human wave rising before it breaks on the shore. But all at once the arrival of the train galvanised everyone. Officials dashed from their offices like so many greyhounds bursting from their traps. Chai wallahs rattled their cups and kettles. Food hawkers pushed their trolleys to the edge of the platform where they could be right up against the train windows to sell their sweet confections to the people inside. Stiff-limbed passengers stretched aching muscles and coughed and hacked like old men getting up in the morning. And people who had come to see friends and relatives off started wishing fond farewells at the tops of their voices. Any notion of a bygone, romantic age of rail travel I may have harboured was quickly dispelled by the sight of the Avadh Express as it slid alongside the platform. It was big, dirty, rusty, smelly and noisy, and was painted a grubby brown in colour.

The great age of steam had all but died out in India and these hulking great diesels had clearly taken over.

It eventually came to a halt and I went in search of my carriage. I quickly found the second class, air-conditioned sleepers near the centre of the train, and just as the Assistant Vigilance Officer had predicted there were three of them. Right by the doors were lists of names sellotaped to the sides of the carriages, and by the names someone had scrawled in blue biro the numbers of the berths allotted to each passenger. I checked the first carriage but there was no mention of my name. I shouldered my way down to the second carriage; no easy task when you're carrying a heavy backpack and battling against a couple of hundred people all intent in going in the opposite direction. Here it was the same story. This had to be a case of third time lucky, I thought, as I approached the third carriage. I quickly scanned the list of names and was no little perturbed to find that mine didn't figure amongst any of them. Hmmmm, clearly a job for the Assistant Vigilance Officer, and I was about to head back and seek his assistance when a man in a grubby and threadbare blue uniform stepped off the train. He wore a frayed armband over his bicep that said, Conductor. He was five feet and a few inches tall, pot-bellied, balding and had gapped and yellow teeth. However, not even a Bollywood heart-throb could have attracted more adoration from a fawning public. As soon as he set foot on the platform he was besieged by a horde of passengers all waving tickets in the air and pleading to be assigned berths. There was nothing to do but join the throng.

I started out by politely waiting my turn, and as a result got myself steadily pushed back to the back of the crowd. Train conductors, I was fast discovering, were very important people. They held the immediate fate of thousands of passengers in the palms of their hands, and it soon became obvious that mine warranted no special attention whatsoever. In desperation, and for once forgetting all English sensibilities about the politeness of queuing, I pushed myself to the front and placed myself in front of the man.

"I have a reservation for this train, but I can't find my name on any of the lists," I said, holding out my reservation. He glanced at it and consulted the scraps of computer printed paper that were attached to a clipboard he held in his right hand. He flicked through the sheets one by one, shook his head and said, "I have no reservation for you."

"But you must have, this reservation was booked weeks ago. In England," I added for good measure in the vain hope that a reference to the old mother land might make a difference.

"No name on list, no reservation," he said waving the clipboard in the air for emphasis.

"Can you check your list again please, my name has to be on there somewhere," I said, beginning to get a little irate.

"No reservation, no reservation," was all he kept repeating in the finest traditions of the Indian mantra. He didn't even bother to look at the list again. The locomotive gave an urgent whistle and the conductor stepped back onto the train, leaving me and a large number of other disgruntled passengers as it slowly began to pull away. There I was standing on a station platform in Agra, in the middle of the night, with a valid ticket in my hand, watching my train disappear into the night and taking my complete India itinerary with it. There was only one thing for it. I hoisted my backpack and sprinted like hell down the platform after what I was sure was my sleeper carriage. Shoeshine boys and chai wallahs scattered in all directions as I careered violently left and right under the weight of my wildly swinging backpack as I steadily gained on the departing train. In the immortal words of Wellington after the Battle of Waterloo, it was a damned close-run thing, but somehow I managed to haul myself on to the last sleeper carriage only yards before the platform ran out. I was aboard, but I had nowhere to go. I peeked round the corner of the door and into the carriage. It was completely open plan. Down one side sleeping berths bolted to the wall were arranged in threes, one above the other, and pointed outwards into the main body of the carriage. They were arranged in what I suppose could be called cubicles, each one being of six berths, and which separated one from the other by a thin, blue curtain. Along the other side the berths were arranged one above the other but running along the length of the carriage. They were also separated by the same blue curtains. Private, they weren't. People were busy sorting themselves out in the confined space, and I reasoned that it was best to let them get on with it, and then hopefully a process of elimination should reveal my berth. In the meantime I stood in the cramped space outside the carriage by the toilets wandering what to do next while eyeing a dirty patch of floor as the only possible corner in which to doss down for the night.

I had been standing there for what must have been ten minutes when a soldier ambled by. I later worked out that he was on train duty, it being the norm on India Rail to have armed guards patrolling the carriages. I never worked out if I was reassured by this or made to feel nervous. Anyway, he took one look at me, in that up and down sort of way that all officials have and which make you feel you forgot to put your clothes on that morning.

"Can I see your reservation ticket please," he asked me. I handed it over. He took one look at it and said, "This is a valid ticket, why do you not have a berth?" I started to like him. Then I explained that the conductor had ignored my pleas and that I was hoping that a berth would reveal itself when everyone else got sorted.

"Please wait here," he said, "I will go and talk to the conductor." I started to really like him. Five minutes later he was back with the conductor who motioned to me to follow him. We negotiated our way through the carriage, gingerly picking our way over outstretched legs and the piles of luggage that littered the narrow gaps between the berths. Flashing eyes and shy smiles loomed out of the darkness and greeted my progress as I tripped, stumbled and apologised my way towards the next carriage. The conductor stopped and did another bout of cross referencing on his list, then grabbed my ticket and scribbled the number forty-six on to it and stuffed it back in my hand. It turned out to be a top one in a "cubicle" of six and was located right at the end of the carriage by the door. I stowed my backpack underneath the bottom bunk and clambered up and settled myself in for the night. A few minutes later the conductor returned with a sheet, a thin blanket and a pillow that held about as much stuffing as a cricket bat. But I didn't mind, I had a berth. The sheet and blanket were only tokens really as everyone slept fully clothed anyway. I zipped up my fleece, stretched out and lay flat on my back. The curved ceiling of the carriage was only 18 inches from the tip of my nose, and slap bang in the middle of it, right above my face, was an electric fan. Whether sleep would come or not did not seem to matter a great deal. I was on my way and tomorrow, at 6.40am, I would arrive in Lucknow. I celebrated by cracking open the packet of biscuits I had bought and washed them down with sips of bottled mineral water. Thankfully the water was still quite cool. I dozed off to the gentle swaying of the carriage and the sound of the wheels racketing over the tracks, which was intermingled with the occasional snores and sighs of my fellow passengers.

One little footnote though, thanks to the ceiling fan recycling every germ and bug being exhaled by every passenger throughout the carriage, and blowing them straight into my face from a distance of less than a couple of feet, I woke up the next morning with a streaming cold. It stayed with me throughout my entire stay in India.

Next morning I didn't exactly get off to a flying start. The rolling clickety-clack of the train had worked its magic and I had slept heavily and awoke to realise that we had arrived. People and their luggage were heading for the door, guards were shouting, and on the platform outside porters were calling out for custom. I checked my watch, almost 7.00am. I sat up bolt upright in bed and promptly slumped back down again. The resounding clang as my head struck the carriage roof echoed around the carriage rather like the large gong that introduced those old J. Arthur Rank films. Mildly concussed, I struggled to focus on the large sign that stood on the platform opposite my grimy, yellow streaked window. Slowly it began to swim into focus – Lucknow. I had arrived. But how long the train had been standing at the platform I had no idea. More importantly, it could be about to depart for the next station at any second. In a blind panic I clawed on my shoes, dug out my backpack and shouldered it and bolted for the door. Of course, I needn't have bothered, because as soon as I hit the platform I realised that Lucknow was the end of the line.

Then, for once in my life, and certainly for the first time since I had started travelling, I had a sensible idea. While I was at the station I thought it would be a good idea to go to the ticket reservation office and confirm my berth for the next stage of my onward journey to Varanasi. All the platforms emerged on to a central concourse. I threaded my way through the throng of hawkers, beggars and passengers, and joined a short queue of other passengers at the ticket office. Five minutes later I was standing at the little window being greeted by a smiling Indrail official. I reached into my top pocket and no reservations. Either they had fallen out of my pocket, or more likely they had accidentally got discarded in my haste to get off the train. I ran back down the platform to find my carriage, but could I? There were only three sleeper carriages but somehow they all conspired to look completely different to the one I had spent the night in. I went into all three of them, found the top bunk by the doorway in each one and frantically threw off the blankets and sheets and checked the floors, but to no avail. At least I still had my Indrail pass which entitled me to travel on any train, but the loss of the berth reservations meant that there was a very good chance that I'd be sleeping on the floor. Back at the ticket office the smiling Indrail official told me that I was in luck.

"Lucknow is being a major terminus," he told me. Pride positively beamed from his every feature and his head wobbled on his shoulders the way nodding dogs do in the backs of cars. "We are having a computer terminal centre here. Very edge cutting," he assured me. "You only have to be going to the big office and they will issue you with new reservations. Very quick, quick."

I thanked him and made my way to the office which was only a short walk from the station. The ticket office may have been "very edge cutting" but like everything else in India it was also "very form filling". Fortunately, I had made a note of all the trains I was booked on and was able to fill in the forms quite quickly. I handed them over and a man started looking them up on the computer.

"Ah, here are being your bookings, Sir." He tilted the screen round so that I could indeed confirm that he had found the right ones. I congratulated him on a job well done. "Now we will be printing off reservation tickets just like you had before." And with that he punched a key and nothing happened. He punched it again, still nothing. "Oh dear," he said, "there is being a big problem with the printer I am thinking." After a couple of minutes of fruitless button punching he asked for my Indrail pass and scribbled the carriage numbers and reserved berths on the back of it. "Many apologies, Sir, but this will be having to do, and nobody will be having your berths on these trains anyway. Just be telling the conductors on the trains and everything will be being hokey-cokey." Judging by my first run in with an Indrail conductor, I can't say as I shared his sense of confidence.

I would be staying in Lucknow for two nights and I had pre-booked a room at the Gomti Hotel, a cheap-ish, mid range hotel that stood in a leafy side street just a five minutes walk off the main Mahatma Ghandi Road. In booking the cheap Gomti Hotel I had hoped to rub shoulders with other itinerant travellers and swap travellers tales. But it soon became apparent that I was the only such animal. I had managed to book myself in during the two days when the place was playing host to a photocopier convention. Salesman from all over India mingled everywhere discussing the different merits of printing rates and different types of toner. So instead of having conversations with bearded ex-hippies about ashrams, I would find myself in the bar being asked if I knew whether the photocopiers in the UK featured the new multi-cartridge loading system.

The next morning I needed to change some money. At reception they gave me directions to the nearest branch of the Bank of Allahabad, which was a short walk away on the Mahatma Ghandi Road. I walked past the bank half a dozen times before I realised that the large building site which occupied the address I had been given was in fact the aforementioned bank. I stepped over some planks of wood and dodged round a concrete mixer and headed for what I guessed was the entrance. I wasn't wrong. Inside a concierge in a military looking uniform smiled and saluted. A hand written sign stuck to the wall told me that the foreign exchange bureau was up a flight of bare concrete stairs that was still being built and was devoid of any hand rails. I gingerly made my way up while all around me workmen hammered and sawed and drilled. I emerged into an open space to find half a dozen people sitting behind desks. The walls were only half erected, the floor was bare boards but it did have a roof of sorts. Naked electric wires sprouted from the walls in clumps, which I swear at one moment I heard throb. It looked like in India's headlong rush towards economic development, health and safety was somewhat lagging behind. Even so, the shiny, new computer terminals on the desks seemed to be working though. Business was brisk. When there existed the serious prospect of some hard currency to be exchanged, the attitude seemed to be nothing should stand in the way of a speedy transaction. I handed over $100 in traveller's cheques, which despite the presence of the desktop computer terminals, inspired a lot of duplicate and triplicate form filling. I was given a receipt which I was told I had to take downstairs and hand over to get my rupees. I picked my way carefully down the open plan staircase, careful to step over electric drills, spirit levels and the other assorted detritus of building construction. The smiling concierge seemed surprisingly keen to see me again, perhaps he was relieved that I'd made it safely back down again. So much so that he personally escorted me over to the appropriate window. The young man there took my receipt and started counting out piles of rupee notes, a process which took almost as long as the form filling session upstairs. I left with a wad of notes the size and weight of a brick.

What the Gomti lacked in old world atmosphere was certainly more than made up for by the Residency. Lucknow was one of the three sites where, what we in England call the Indian Mutiny but which Indian history refers to as the First War of Independence, took place. The others were Delhi and Cawnpore. In 1867, the British Residency had been a proud and noble looking cantonment, a small Victorian city state within a sprawling Indian metropolis. During the Mutiny the Residency was completely cut off and besieged for six months. Those trapped inside included women and children. It was the British Empire's Alamo. I visited the Residency in the late afternoon, when the light was kind. It bathed the battered building in a soft light, as if trying to smooth the scars etched into the walls left by the shell bursts and the pockmarks of the countless bullet holes. It was a strangely peaceful place at this time of day. For the people of Lucknow the Residency is a park, a green space and a haven of quiet and solitude. Lovers walked hand in hand through the banyan trees, students lay on the well kept lawns swotting from text books, and young-sters ran in the shade of the ruins flying kites. The ruins themselves stood much as they were when Sir Colin Campbell led the 997 survivors of the siege out of the battered remains all those years ago.

By the end of the siege most of the perimeter buildings had been completely flattened. On those battered remnants that still stood, the effects of grape and shell were still plain to see. I entered through the Bailee Gate, which was the original entrance to the cantonment. As such it had played an all-important symbolic as well as strategic role throughout the siege and despite terrible losses was resolutely defended and never taken. A hundred yards back from the Bailee Gate stood Dr Fayrer's house. He had been one of the key figures in the story of the siege. The house must have once been a grand, Palladian looking affair. Two days after the siege began it is where the Residency's commander, Sir Henry Lawrence, was brought to die. In a show of typical British pluck, he had refused to leave his headquarters in the main Residency building and was mortally wounded when a shell exploded in his office. The once elegant Banqueting Hall was now only a shadow of its former glory. Its plaster flesh had been stripped away all those years ago by what must have been a blistering bombardment, which had blasted it to its structural bare bones. Fragments and details still remained though. I caught a glimpse of a marble fireplace and an elegant piece of corning. Walking through the ruins staring at the walls it was easy to imagine the grand balls and receptions that took place here, the swagger and pomp that only the British Raj at its zenith could have mustered. My guide book told me that the Banqueting Hall spent its last days as a makeshift hospital. It wasn't hard to imagine what pain, suffering, and ultimately death, was endured here in what must have become a charnel house. Deprived of food, water and even the most basic medicines, this is where the women held their loved ones as they wasted away and died for want of a cup of brackish water. Survivors who kept diaries of the siege say it was the plight of the children that was the most distressing. Those who endured the siege did so in the blistering heat of an Indian summer.

The principal target during the siege was the main Residency building itself. The shattered walls still stand, testimony to the punishment rendered by 87 days of ceaseless shelling. Only its structural shell remained, but it still caught the evening light majestically. Stripped of its stucco and plaster by remorseless fire, the blood red inner brickwork was revealed like wounds laid bare.

The Mutiny was eventually suppressed and the Residency retaken. The retributions meted out by the victorious British were as brutal as they were barbaric. I spent the last hour quietly walking through the regimental graveyard where many of the victims of the siege are interned. I was brought up in a small village in Hertfordshire. On summer evenings, I wouldn't be the only one strolling through the village churchyard and cemetery. I was always reassured and comforted to see the family plots with generations of a single family lying side by side, their births, marriages and deaths listed on the gravestones. For me these places serve to underline the gentle continuity of English rural life. They ordain a natural order. But the cemetery in Lucknow was different, and it was the dates on the gravestones that brought the point home. They recorded the fact that of the many hundreds of people who died in the siege, many of them were very young.

I returned to the Gomti Hotel, and by 6 o'clock I was showered, packed and ready to go. My next train, the exotically named Kashi Vishwanath Express, didn't leave Lucknow until 10.30 so I decided to kill an hour or so by finding somewhere to have something to eat. The Royal Palace was a lively little restaurant five minutes walk from the Gomti Hotel, which made it within backpack carrying walking distance. When I arrived the place was crowded. Most of the restaurant was taken up by three long tables that stretched the entire length of the room, and where people just plonked themselves down and ordered. I did the same and ordered a murgh korma.

I figured it was a ten minutes taxi ride to the station but gave myself half an hour all the same, just to be on the safe side. The Royal Palace was on the main Mahatma Gandhi Road, which was always busy so I knew I would be able to pick up a cab right outside the door. Or so I thought. When I emerged into the totally deserted street I momentarily thought I had walked into an Indian version of High Noon. If a tumbleweed had rolled across the street I would not have been surprised. Normally, the wide road thronged with traffic bumper to bumper, now there was not a soul astir, which was very spooky because that simply never happens in India. I stood in the middle of the road for a couple of minutes before I heard the rhythmic squeaking of an approaching cycle rickshaw. I flagged it down, bundled my backpack up on to the seat and climbed up beside it. Fortunately, the receptionist at the Gomti had told me that the station I wanted was known locally as "Charbar", so I was able to give him my destination.

We headed off into the pitch darkness. No lights shone from the deserted shops and offices we passed along the way and even the streetlights had been turned off. Only the slowly pitching body movement of the rickshaw wallah as he worked at the pedals was dimly discernible in the darkness. And it was pitch dark. The only thing that told me I was actually moving was the occasional jolt I felt whenever we went over a pothole. It was completely silent, too. Then suddenly, out of the inky black of the Indian night, the station swam into view. It was with a sense of some relief that I recognised the Reservations Centre, where they had sorted me out the day I arrived. How well it had done its job I was about to find out. So relieved was I to be there with five minutes to spare that I passed the rickshaw wallah a 50 rupees note. I picked my way through the station concourse, which was littered with sleeping bodies lying on the marble floor wrapped up in shawls and blankets. Every so often the tinny PA system would blare out the expected arrival of a train, but the sleepers seemed oblivious to the racket and slept on, catlike in their seeming comfort on the cold, unforgiving marble slabs, bare brown legs sticking out of the folds of their clothes. Every square inch was occupied, and if not by passengers then by the stockpiles of their luggage. Not even the rolling thunder made by the creaking, rusting diesels, dragging endless lines of carriages packed with dark faced humanity, seemed to disturb the sleeping carpet of passengers. I picked my way through the bodies to a lighted window. A railway official was sitting dozing behind the glass. He jolted awake as I tapped on the window.

"Which platform do I want for the Varanasi train?" I asked him.

"You are after wanting platform number three," he said, stirring himself into action as a queue of passengers began to form behind me. When I descended on to the platform it was a completely different story. It was crowded with people who were upright in eager anticipation of the expected train. I wandered up and down the platform and spotted a sign that was headed, RESERVATIONS, and was illuminated by a bare strip light. Long lists of the now all-too-familiar computer printouts were pinned to it bearing the names of passengers who had berths reserved for them on all the incoming trains. I scanned the lists but my name didn't appear on any of them. Here we go again I thought, I'll just have to see what happens. I elbowed my way on to a patch of platform to stand on and waited.

Now St. Christopher may have been given his marching orders as the patron saint of travellers, but there is obviously some divine presence up there who continues to look after our interests. It must have been this guiding hand that placed me next to two young Indian men in their early twenties. Typically, it did not take one of them long to strike up a conversation. The one who did all the talking was short and plump and his name was Amitabh. The quiet one was called Anoop. They were two friends who were on their way to play baseball of all things. We chit-chatted back and fourth about life in England and Lucknow, and being Indians they were potty about cricket. We were discussing the various reasons for the demise of our national game when Amitabh raised a hand, cocked an ear and assumed that staring into the middle distance look that afflicts only those who have just heard something they deem important.

"I am very sorry Bob to be interrupting you," he said. "Many apologies but they have just made an announcement about the Varanasi train. It is to be arriving on platform six."

"Oh," I said, and bending down to shoulder my backpack, "well, it was nice talking to you both, and I hope…"

Another machine gun burst of Hindi hammered out of the tannoy. His face relaxed. "Very sorry, my mistake, my English is sometimes not so well."

"Not at all," I reassured him, relieved that I was still on course so to speak. "As I was saying, it was…"

Patiently Amithab raised his hand to interrupt me, "Very sorry Bob, you are having to excuse me again." I deferred. "They are saying that the Varanasi train is about to depart from platform six."

"What!!!!!!!" I shook their outstretched hands and wished them hasty farewells, and legged it for the stairs. I arrived on platform six a couple of minutes later heaving, sweating and no little agitated. In a glance I took in the fact that there were still plenty of passengers milling about the platform and the food hawkers were still doing a brisk trade, handing little foil dishes and morsels wrapped in banana leaves through the windows of the carriages. I gambled that time was still on my side. I headed up the platform in search of the second class sleeper carriages. I found one, and there by the door stuck to the outside of the carriage with sellotape was a computer printout list of berth reservations. This time surely, I thought, as I ran my eyes down the list. Lots of names but not one of them was mine. A train whistle blew adding to my mounting panic. I dug out my passenger reservation number but that did not correlate with any of the numbers listed either. The platform was noticeably thinning so I headed towards the rear of the train. All the carriages were of the third class variety, packed with passengers on wooden benches. An Indian gentleman who happened to be passing by picked up on my obvious distress. I think he had just seen someone off.

"Excuse me, can I be of assistance." he said.

"I have a second class sleeper berth reserved somewhere on this train," I said, "but for the life of me I can't work out where."

"You will find the second class sleeper carriages towards the front of the train," he said, and gently grabbed me by the arm and walked me in the right direction. He found the designated carriage and I had to resist the temptation to kiss him on both cheeks as he waved me goodbye. I climbed aboard with a similar sense of relief to what I imagine was experienced by the survivors of the Titanic when they were hauled into a passing life boat. A carriage attendant stood just inside the door and I barked the number of my berth at him. As he led me down the central corridor the train chugged into life.

Once again I had been assigned the top bunk but this time I was sharing with an Indian family. The top bunks had not been pulled down as yet and were still flush to the wall. This meant I had to join my fellow passengers sitting on the two lower bunks which faced each other like benches across a gap of no more than a couple of feet. The father shuffled up and let me squeeze into the space by the window. His wife sat opposite him and was bent over a small primus stove like boy scouts used to use when out camping. The husband was dressed in casual western clothes while his wife wore a sari and her hair was covered by a long shawl which was wrapped round her shoulders. They greeted me wordlessly but kindly with nods of their heads.

If they were disappointed to have their little home from home disturbed by the sudden appearance of a stranger from a strange land, they had the good grace not to let it show. Their three children stared at me with wide eyed amazement, and the father gently scolded them for being rude, but he knew he had a losing battle on his hands. It was obvious they didn't speak English, so instead the physical language of polite family culture took its place.

As the mother busied herself preparing their evening meal I took out my note book and started writing down notes. The eldest boy, who was about seven, was transfixed by my jottings, enough to overcome his initial shyness and he clambered up on the seat next to his father beside me to get a closer look at what the strange man was doing. After a couple of minutes I turned to a fresh page, tilted the note book towards my young travelling companion and started to draw a crude rendition of an elephant. At first my formless scribbling meant nothing to him but as it began to take shape he looked up at his father and started talking fifteen to the dozen. By the time I added a tusk with a pronounced artistic flourish, (and yes I know elephants have two but I'm no Picasso and this was a simple profile) he was twitching with excitement. Now it was his turn. I turned to a fresh page and handed him the note book and pen. His rendition of an elephant took him all of five minutes, and despite the odd wobbly line resulting from whenever the train trundled over a particularly dodgy set of points, his drawing of an elephant was infinitely superior to mine. He even put one of those palanquin type things on its back that maharajas were wont to travel in, which personally I thought was cheating. Not to be outdone by a seven year old, I drew a camel. And not to be beaten by a middle-aged foreigner who couldn't even speak Hindi, the seven year old drew a camel pulling a cart piled high with stuff. I think the "stuff" was supposed to be fruit, but as he was working in the medium of blue biro perhaps the idea was a little over ambitious. Either that or as an artist he was a form and line over colour man. When I drew a house he drew a mosque complete with minarets. And so it went on until his mother called time for tea.

She laid out plates of pastries and *pakoras*, together with large slabs of *naan* bread and little pots of sauces. She took out plastic plates from a bag at her feet and handed them round to the children and without a second thought handed me one as well. Normally, I would have been terribly English and my first reaction would have been to politely refuse, but it happened so fast and so naturally I was taken completely unawares, and truth be told, completely charmed by the gesture. After the meal the parents got the children ready for bed, not an easy task in a confined space about the size of a few telephone boxes pushed together.

Without a word the mother simply plonked her baby on my lap as she packed up the meal things and got the children into some night clothes. I sat there for a good ten minutes with the warm little bundle gurgling happily in my arms while Dad made up the beds and Mum poured water into a bowl on the floor and washed the children's faces.

Ablutions completed, she reached across and took the baby giving me a warm smile of thanks. Having sorted out the bunks for his family, the father pulled down my top bunk for me as well and indicated with a nod of his head that this was where I would be sleeping. Once they were all tucked in, I got myself ready for bed as well, which involved no more than pulling my fleece on and climbing fully clothed up onto my bunk. But before I did I tore out the pages of the drawings my little friend and I had done together and gave them to him. I lay awake thinking that this was the true magic of travelling by rail in India, you simply became part of a village on wheels, and the culture dictated that everyone being a fellow traveller meant that we were all the same and should help each other out. George would have immediately recognised this caring sense of community and would have heartily approved. Perhaps there were more similarities to Bangalore, Bihar, Bengal and the world of Bedford Falls than first met the eye, I wondered, before I let the gently rocking of the train on the tracks do its thing.

The train was due to arrive at Varanasi the next morning at 5.40. I woke at 6.15. I leaned out of my bunk and checked down below. The berths were deserted, the family had left, no doubt when we stopped at a station during the night. I clambered down and sat by the window and peered out across the empty, flat countryside, which was lit by the early morning sunlight. Men in shirts and red print dhotis walked to their patches of land carrying long handled agricultural tools on their shoulders, where they would toil all day. Fires were bursting into life in the small hamlets we past that hugged the tracks. Twenty minutes later we pulled into Varanasi station.

I emerged from the station into an open space that was filled with rickshaws and taxis. Very few people got off the early morning train so I was surrounded by a larger, buzzier swarm of rickshaw wallahs than usual. As per usual I was defenceless in front of the most persistent of them. I gave him the name of my hotel and he tried the old "Oh, but it's not there anymore" scam. This is one of the more popular ones they try on you in India. Either the hotel does not exist, or was burnt down last night. "But not to making worry, I take you to good hotel, much better and very cheap, cheap. It's owned by my cousin." I stuck to my guns and when he realised I was not having any of it, and with a gracious smile, he agreed to take me to where I wanted to go, as if the previous conversation had never existed. We settled on a price and he led me to his auto rickshaw. Actually, it wasn't his rickshaw. He was the front-of-house man and he climbed in beside the driver and I got in the back. The streets were relatively empty at that time of the morning. Just a few Ambassador taxis taking bosses to work and the odd bus and rickshaw. We putt-putted along for half an hour and then turned into the old cantonment area.

"This is being most honourable legacy of British Raj, Sir," my rickshaw wallah told me before giving me a short history lesson. He told me that cantonments could be found in cities all over India where the British had been. They were rich ghettos where they built their villas, bungalows and offices. The first thing I noticed was that they had manicured grass verges. As something of a throw back to its imperial past, the cantonment area in Varanasi was where all the upmarket hotels were to be found. They all stood next to one another like prized china in a display cabinet. I had booked a room in one of the most modern of them. It was luxurious and totally soulless. But after the Gomti and an overnight sleeping on the train I was in the mood for a bit of luxury. It felt strange being in a smart hotel for a change. Over a cup of coffee I skimmed my Lonely Planet guidebook and mentally sketched out an itinerary. The object of any visit to Varanasi, for Hindus and travellers alike, is to go to the bathing *ghats*. The best time to visit them, my guidebook told me, was at dawn. At reception I asked the man behind the desk about ordering a taxi to take to the *ghats* at dawn the next day.

"This is not being a problem, Sir," he reassured me, "I have a cousin who is driving very fine taxi. I will phone him now and he will be picking you up here at the hotel tomorrow, very early, Sir."

Next morning I was up at 5.15. It was pitch dark and for once strangely cold as I stepped outside where my driver was waiting for me. Once again I climbed into the back of an aged Ambassador taxi. We drove through the normally crowded streets, but at this early hour they were strangely almost deserted. For once the tourists outnumbered the Indians as we made our various ways in cycle and auto rickshaws, and taxis, down to the river. As the Ambassador chugged through the narrow streets I looked out and saw people huddled under blankets crouching over small fires they had built by the roadside. They extended their hands to the small flames eager to suck in any heat. Others continued to sleep in doorways, putting off to the final moment when they awoke to face another day of struggle surviving on the street.

It was still dark as we arrived at the river but already a crowd of hawkers were busy preying on the tourists as soon as they emerged from their taxis and rickshaws. My taxi driver told me he had a cousin who would take me out on his boat and would give me "very good price". No sooner had I agreed than the cousin in question miraculously appeared out of no-where. The boatman led me down to the water's edge where he took me to a large wooden rowing boat. Other boatmen were filling their boats with upwards of twenty people so when my boatman and I haggled over the price, which we fixed at six hundred rupees, I guessed I had paid well over the odds. But if it meant I had the boat to myself for what I hoped was going to be a highly spiritual, once-in-a-lifetime experience, so be it. I handed over the money and received a *puja* in return. This was a small lighted candle, cradled in a banana leaf, which my boatman told me to float on the river as an offering to the gods. Cradling my lighted puja in my cupped hands, and shielding the delicate flame from the breeze that was rippling the surface of the dark water, we rowed out into the darkness.

A three quarter moon hung overhead in a starless sky and a faint glow began to lighten the horizon over the eastern bank. We were the first boat out that morning and the only sound was the creaking and splash of the oars as my boatman rhythmically pulled at them.

I already knew that the city of Varanasi is the holiest of holies for Hindus and the spiritual soul of the country. But my boatman, who spoke very good English, was able to enlighten me further. "Varanasi is the city of Shiva," he told me as he continued to pull steadily at the heavy, wooden oars. "Shiva takes many forms and is the Destroyer and the Lord of the Dance. When you see a statue of a god with snakes around his neck, this is Shiva." But for such a fearsome character he was very popular with the ladies apparently. "He is also being the wife of Parvati and is a very good husband," said my boatman. "My wife is always making offerings to Shiva to make me a better husband."

He told me that Hindus believe that they are born, they die, and are reborn again in a constant cycle of reincarnation. How well you live your life determines what you come back as. Devote your life to good works and study and you might be lucky to come back as someone happier and better off than you are now. It is a constant cycle. "To die in Varanasi," he said, "is to break the circle of death and rebirth and achieve nirvana."

As we headed slowly up river we led a small flotilla of other boats, some crammed with a dozen or more people, who followed silently in our wake. The towering edifices of the *ghats*, and the temples above them, slowly began to loom out of the darkness as the first flickers of dawn pierced the gloom.

"The *ghats* are the stone steps that lead down to the river," the boatman said. All was quiet on the river. Looking back over my shoulder I could see the silhouettes of other boats, barely discernible shapes against the dark backdrop of the river, and were picked out by the flickering flames of the puja offerings being held in hundreds of pairs of cupped hands. Our flotilla of boats had set off from the *Desawamedh Ghat*, one of the busiest ghats situated at the centre of the great arc of them that stretched for two miles along the western shore of the river. The creaking of oars to my right announced the presence of another boat that drew alongside. I vaguely discerned a gap-toothed grin below a grubby white cloth coiled round a dark head. It was a hawker selling small earthenware bottles with ornate stoppers stuffed into their necks.

"They are for taking some of the holy water of the Ganges," my boatman explained before shooing him away. Even out on the river in the chill of pre-dawn there was no escaping the hawkers.

After 20 minutes leisurely stroking at his oars, my boatman turned the boat around. As we headed down river, with the *ghats* on our left, to our right the sky began to lighten. We glided through the water a little more quickly now that we were with the current. The temples took on more discernible shapes as they emerged out of the inky night into a ghostly half dawn. They were majestic when seen from the river. The sun was still below the horizon away to our right but was throwing its light high into the sky overhead. Bathers were already waist deep in the river waiting for the first rays to touch them.

"Many *sadhus* come to bathe at Varanasi," said my boatman, "they pour blessings on their heads when they bathe in the holy waters of the river at dawn."

I had already seen a few of these strange holy men. They wore next to nothing, just a scrap of cloth to cover their modesty which was usually saffron, the colour of the dawn. They carried few if any possessions and were made even more conspicuous by their appearances. Often they had heads of unwashed hair that hung long over their shoulders, and beards that grew in bizarre profusions. It wasn't unusual for them to cover their near naked bodies in grey ash.

"Many of the *sadhus* were wealthy men before," said my boatman. "They renounce all worldly possessions, and even leave their families, to follow the way to true enlightenment."

For the bathers standing in the shallows of the Ganges, it was not hard to believe that for each and every one of them they had lived for this moment. We were 50 yards out from the ghats when that moment came. The sun rose above the eastern horizon and sent a shaft of intense golden light across the water, momentarily turning the water of the Ganges the colour of burnished copper. The sunlight flooded up over the *ghats* like a golden wave, drenching the carved stone steps and the temples above them in its amber glow. As it washed over the *sadhus* and the other bathers who stood waist deep in the water facing the rising sun, they pressed their palms together and bowed their heads, while others quietly slipped below the surface of the holy waters immersing themselves completely in its watery embrace. All at once, and as if they were being conducted by a celestial presence, the bells of the temples rang out in a clanging cacophony of chimes that echoed round the *ghats* and out to where we lay in the river slowly drifting in the current, my boatman having shifted his oars moments before. I turned to ask him something but the question died on my lips. He too was bowed in prayer, and he rocked gently back and forth with his palms pressed together. The sun rose swiftly and the panorama of Varanasi, as seen from the river, changed from deep gold to pale yellow within seemingly a matter of moments. The peel of the temple bells faded away as the sounds of the city beyond the river slowly coming to life swelled. Varanasi was waking up to another day.

It didn't take me long to realise Varanasi is a very spiritual place. The spirit of commercialism courses through it. Nothing represented this better than the cousin scam. Whenever you wanted something, if the person you were talking to couldn't do it, you could bet your bottom rupee that he had a cousin who could, and one that guaranteed him a commission on the deal. You only had to stand a few seconds in any one place and in no time at all you would be besieged by all manner of street hawkers selling their services or wares. The most prolific were the barbers and head massage wallahs, followed closely by the post card and souvenir sellers. For a Hindu, dying at Varanasi may mean the end of the cycle of death and rebirth. But for a tourist, stepping off the boat and back on to dry land meant that the cycle of commercialism started up all over again.

The other "must see" in Varanasi is the Golden Temple, one of the most revered places of worship for Hindus. It is located in the heart of the city, and can only be reached on foot through the most intricate maze of narrow back streets. The temple gets its name from its tall, intricately carved domes, which are gold plated. It would have been impossible to find on my own so a guide was essential. "I have a cousin who can take you," said my boatman, and dashed off. He returned a few minutes later with a smiling, young man who bore as much family resemblance to my boatman as Boris Karloff did to Brad Pitt. He asked for 50 rupees and we entered into negotiations. To be honest, despite the terrible poverty I was beginning to get a bit brassed off with all the chiselling that went on. You couldn't go anywhere, or do anything, without entering into a major haggling session or dishing out backsheesh. After a while, it wasn't so much the money as the principle of the thing. I always felt I was being ripped off and that I was having my intelligence insulted. Suffice to say, that after five minutes of ruthless negotiating I handed over a crisp, new 50 rupees note and off we went.

From the Desawamedh Ghat it was a short walk through the twisting alleyways. We wound our way through the narrow streets going deeper and deeper into the old city. We passed shops, which were no more than small kiosks, where shopkeepers sat cross-legged on mats surrounded by whatever it was they were selling: pots and pans, batteries, music cassettes, fresh fruit, saris. Passers-by jostled us in the narrow streets, and at one point we had to backtrack down the lane we were walking along when a cow appeared at the other end ambling towards us, in a slow motion version of running with the bulls at Pamplona.

We were walking along a particularly narrow street when my guide stopped me and pointed high up and over to my right. Over a rough brick wall, which was half covered in flaking plaster, I caught a glimpse of one of the gold plated domes of the temple.

"Non-Hindus are not allowed to enter the temple," said my guide, "and you are not allowed to be taking photographs."

Before I had a chance to ball him out for obviously conning me into thinking that I would be able to at least see the temple, he grabbed me by the elbow and ushered me into a small silk shop. The shopkeeper approached us and he and my guide put their heads together and started talking in hushed tones. I knew what was coming. My guide turned to me and with a broad smile on his face told me that the shopkeeper was his cousin, and that he had agreed to let me and my guide go upstairs where there was a window overlooking the temple courtyard.

"He is saying this is only being 50 rupees," said my guide. I promptly fished out a 50 rupee note and handed it over to the shopkeeper, who grabbed it with the speed of a striking cobra and it disappeared into his pocket.

The three of us went through to the back of the shop and emerged into an open courtyard the size of two telephone boxes that had been knocked through. The shopkeeper led us up a rickety staircase that snaked up the walls of the courtyard towards a doorway that stood under the overhanging roof. I had to stoop low to get through it and we emerged into a small, bare room. "Come," said the shopkeeper as he gestured for me to follow him over to the window in the opposite wall that overlooked the street. It was covered with a ragged cloth that acted as a curtain. Then, and with all the theatricality of Houdini revealing a death defying marvel, he drew back the curtain.

The temple was not very large and was more of an ornate shrine. Worshippers filed in, ringing the bell at the entrance to announce their presence to the gods. Even from across the street I could easily detect the heady smell of burning incense. The vantage point that the window afforded meant that the outer wall surrounding the temple cut it off about half way up. However, I did get a brief glimpse of the domes in all their golden glory. I say "brief" because a few seconds later the shopkeeper dropped the curtain and demanded another 50 rupees to lift it again. I don't know if the shopkeeper had ever been to Blackpool, but even though the technology was somewhat different the basic principle was the same. It was like a "What the butler saw" machine in a seaside arcade. Just as you got to a tantalising bit the shutters came down and you had to put another coin in the slot. I declined the offer.

The Hindus have Varanasi, the Muslims have Mecca, the Catholics have Rome, the Jews have Jerusalem, and the Buddhists have Sarnath, which, my taxi driver told me, was a short drive out of the city. It was about 10 o'clock in the morning when we arrived and the heat of the day was building nicely. When I stepped out of the car instead of being besieged by a gaggle of guides I was approached by a small man dressed in dark robes and whose head was completely shaved. Kind and intelligent eyes were framed by large black spectacles that gave him a benign, owlish air. He was a Buddhist monk and looked to me like a diddy man version of the Dalai Lama. When he spoke it was in quiet, faultless, heavily accented English. He explained that he lived and worshiped in a nearby monastery and that if I would like he would be happy to escort me around the ruins of Sarnath in return for whatever donation to the monastery I thought his tour warranted. Here was a man cut from the same community conscious cloth as George Bailey if ever there was one, I thought to myself as I accepted his offer. The gentle style of it certainly made for a refreshing change from all the other offers I'd had since I arrived in India.

There was remarkably little left to see. We walked around what seemed a large park of green grass.

"Once there were mighty stone monuments stood here," he said, sweeping a bare arm in the general direction of where we were walking, "but they were all destroyed by Muslim invaders many centuries ago." He went on to explain that the site was rediscovered by an English archaeologist in the nineteenth century. "There used to be many monasteries and places of worship here," he said as we approached a small block of stone buried in the ground, and pointing to it he added, "and now this is all that is left of the Great Emperor Ashok's column."

But what Sarnath may have lacked in monuments it certainly made up for in other ways. Its most revered site was not a monument but a tree, because it was sitting under a tree in the shade here in Sarnath that the Buddha first preached about the middle way, and a direct descendant of that tree has grown on the same site ever since. A small crowd was gathered around it gazing up into its leafy canopy with more awe and reverence than any pilgrim raising his eyes to the dome of St Peter's. It spoke volumes about a religion that renounced the material things of this world wealth and sought peace and contentment through spiritual enlightenment. But not being what could be described as a religious person I thought it was best to leave the worshippers to their perfect moment, although I was grateful for having been allowed the privilege of sharing it, be it fleetingly, for a moment. Walking back to the taxi the monk, having noticed that I was travelling alone, shyly asked me if I was married. I told him that I wasn't. "Ah," he said nodding his head knowingly, "so you can spend your time in quiet meditation. That is good." I didn't have the heart to disabuse him.

"Muslim quarter is very, very famous for very, very fine silks," said my taxi driver, "best quality in all India. Many, many factories making silks in Muslim quarter." Apparently we were on our way to the Muslim quarter, not that I had instructed him to take me there. I knew what was coming next. "You are being very lucky because I am having a cousin of mine who is owning silk factory. Very, very fine silks, very, very cheap price."

A few minutes later we drew up outside a short row of small houses in a back street. He wheeled me straight in. A young, smartly dressed man approached us and my taxi driver launched into an introduction. "This is..." there was a distinct pause as he struggled to remember his so-called cousin's name. Spotting either his embarrassment, or the fact that my taxi driver was about to blow the scam, the young man held out his hand and said, "Good morning, Sir, I am Arun Shamar, and what is being your good name?" I told him and he dutifully produced a business card that told me he was the Liaison Officer. And with that he gently steered me away from my befuddled taxi driver.

"There are ten thousand Muslims living here in Varanasi," he told me. "We all live here in this area, maybe 4,000 homes. Nearly all these people are making silk."

We walked as he talked and I found myself outside by a row of small, terraced houses. "Silks from Varanasi," Arun continued, "are highly prized throughout all of India." He then explained that the raw material comes into the row of houses at one end and a staggering array of silk saris, scarves, bedspreads and cushion covers of exquisite design, colour and quality comes out the other. "First the individual silk strands are dyed," he said and he pointed to where two people stood 50 feet apart. Between them they held what must have constituted thousands and thousands of strands of newly dyed silk strands. Each one was as fine as a single hair on a baby's head. They gently undulated them up and down in warm mid-morning sunshine to dry them, a process which formed a shimmering rainbow.

"They will be doing this all day," he explained as we walked over to one of the houses. We stepped inside into a dark, small, almost bare room where a man was sitting cross-legged on a mat skewering small holes into what looked like a piece of floor tile with a single pronged instrument. Arun explained that this was how the designs were fed into the looms. "Each hole he makes is for a strand of silk which has to be of the right colour." From what I could gather, the designs for the silks were hand-drawn in colour and rendered precisely on to sheets of graph paper. What had been created freehand with pen and ink had to be faithfully transposed into straight lines of different coloured silk, thousands upon thousands of them. This was achieved by transferring the design to a series of punch hole cards that the loom could understand. What the man in front of us was doing was transposing a piece of a design for a silk on to one of these punch cards. To my untrained eye the theory at work seemed to be a lot like a child's join-the-dots drawing, the big difference being that an intricate pattern of a decorated and festooned elephant was far more difficult to manage than a simple line drawing of a kitten.

"It can take many thousands of these cards to make just one silk sari, and all the holes have to be made by hand," said Arun. The work looked slow, painstaking and meticulous. Put a hole in the wrong place and a trained eye could pick out a wrong thread in a finished article at 20 paces. And it wasn't like dropping a stitch at knitting. You couldn't simply unpick it and go back and do it again.

In the main factory, which was another bare room, four men worked ceaselessly on hand looms. Silk saris, in various stages of completion, were stretched across them. No other sound interrupted the flat clacks of the shuttles as they clattered back and forth across the looms. "It can take one of these men up to four months to make a single sari," said Arun.

After the guided tour there was no escaping the showroom. I was ushered in and offered a cup of chai, which I politely refused citing the old traveller's get-out of a dodgy stomach. "Please sit," said Arun indicating a sofa that lined one wall of the room. "This is my home," he informed me, adding, "it is not a shop, I only want to invite you to see the quality or our workmanship. And you are being my honoured guest, of course."

Arun had a technique in studied casualness that he deliberately employed as a sales ploy. And as a salesman he was as smooth as his product. While I sat on the battered sofa Arun took up a position cross-legged on the floor in front of me. From a cupboard he produced a foot high pile of neatly folded silks that he placed in front of him on the carpet. Then, one after the other, he picked each one up by a corner, and with a deft flick of his wrist, sent it billowing up into the air to unfurl and drift back on to the floor in a cascade of dazzling colour. The brightly coloured silk threads caught and bounced the light from the bare strip light over-head. In this way silk after silk burst into a blaze of iridescent colour in front of my eyes. Each one exploded like a silent firework in front of my eyes before drifting down to lie discarded on the threadbare carpet in a crumpled heap. The colours were rich and exotic and the motifs were incredibly detailed and depicted strutting peacocks, elephants in full ceremonial regalia and spectacular floral displays. Then Arun ran through the prices. Not, he assured me, that he was trying to sell them to me but only as a means for me to judge their outstanding quality. They ranged from 12 pounds for a cushion cover up to 120 pounds for a king size bedspread. I had to admit the artistry and workmanship that had gone into them made them extremely good value. Arun sensed that he might be getting somewhere with me and said, "They would cost a lot more in Britisher shops, you know. One of my biggest customers is John Lewis and I am knowing Mr. Lewis personally," he added for good measure. But I let that one go.

The next day I returned to the *ghats* for a leisurely stroll at a more civilized time of day. Whenever possible I always took cycle rickshaws, rather than the motorised ones, primarily because it took longer, and there is not a street in the whole of India that is not worth lingering over, especially in Varanasi. My rickshaw dropped me at the Dasawamedh Ghat and

I walked through the smattering of market stalls selling souvenirs and fresh fruit and continued down to the river. There was a large open concrete space above the *ghat* making it one of the main focal points in Varanasi. An iron balustrade ran along the edge of it overlooking the river. It was a good place to watch the life, and death, of the river drift by. I had not been standing there more than five minutes when the shrouded form of a dead body momentarily broke the surface a few yards in front of me, buoyed upwards no doubt by the expanding gasses trapped inside its body. It floated there for a brief moment like a heavily bandaged mannequin, and then sank slowly without trace again to join the numerous other cadavers silently rotting in the depths of the river below. It was as if he had popped up to take one last look at the world of his old life, and a reminder of how hellish it had all been, before he embarked on his reincarnated next one. Or, if he had been lucky enough to actually die in Varanasi, he could have been on his way to nirvana. His appearance hardly caused a ripple on the surface of the water, and not even a stir amongst my fellow watchers who gazed silently from the bank.

Standing there I quickly became a target for the usual brand of hawkers selling boat rides, head massages, haircuts, and all very good price, of course. I escaped them by walking away downriver along the *ghats*. Yesterday, at dawn, I had seen the ghats in soft focus long shot. Today they appeared in close up and were lit full flood. Buffalo wandered all over the ghats wherever they wanted and shat in the water, right next to the bathers and the women washing clothes. Children frolicked in the shallows, kicked footballs on the steps or sold postcards to passing tourists. The *ghats* rose in steep steps to my left. Yesterday, in silhouette, I had only seen the temples. Now I noticed that bars and cheap guesthouses nestled in amongst them.

The hands that were extended before me in the manner of all beggars were different. They were completely devoid of fingers and thumbs, which had been eaten away by leprosy. She cupped her bandaged stumps together in the vain hope that they could hold a few coins. A quick glance revealed that her feet were as toeless as her hands were fingerless. She tottered rather than walked. She was not much more than five feet tall, her teeth were broken and gapped, and her hair, or what showed of it beneath a filthy cloth wrapped around her head, was grey. She could have been aged anywhere between 30 and 60, such a toll had her pitiable life taken on her. I noticed all this in less that a couple of seconds. As soon as she approached me, arms extended, my automatic pilot kicked in and I stepped aside to avoid her. One is advised to ignore such sad supplicants in India. Give to one and a hundred more appear out of nowhere. What's more, I had read horrific stories of beggars being set upon and robbed when a tourist has been too generous in plain view. Far better, it was argued, to make a donation to a registered charity. Most beggars know that their appeals will fall on deaf ears, but still they try. What choice do they have? They would follow me for ages, often tugging at my sleeve. But this was not an option for the old lady as the terrible disfiguring disease had left her nothing to tug with. Similarly her eaten away feet meant that she could only totter a few paces after me in a pathetic attempt to keep up. In that split second, before I was able to step around her, she stood before me, pleading. What chance did she have in what must be the most competitive industry in India. A few rupees? I didn't even spare her a backward glance. That's what India can do to you after a while, I discovered.

I hurried away from her and made my way towards the burning *ghats*, the funeral pyres of Varanasi. The burning ghats were few in number but could easily be picked out by their telltale wisps of smoke that rose into the air. There was also a sweet, sappy smell that came from the logs that were thrown on to the pyres. The logs stood in tall stacks all around the burning *ghats*, which gave them the appearance of so many lumber yards. A crowd of some 200 people were standing on a terrace that surrounded a central platform where a funeral pyre had obviously been burning for some time. The logs were white hot and had reduced down to where they lay in a pile of white ash. Beyond the terraces stood a Hindu temple, a *mandir*. Monkeys scampered over its domes and chattered wildly to one another, while water buffaloes and feral dogs mingled with the crowd. Everything and everyone was anointed with the sooty, grey ash from the pyre. In a city renowned for dying, death is an everyday occurrence in Varanasi. It also seemed to be a thriving business. A curious example of this, I learnt later, was that one of the burning *ghats* was owned by an untouchable, who was a very rich man. The fact that the lowest caste Hindu could attain such a prominent position, let alone wealth, was highly unusual. It seemed that anyone could make a killing in Varanasi.

I was able to observe the proceedings by maintaining a discreet distance. I stopped some 50 yards from the *ghat* and leant on a low wall overlooking the river. Below me a man in dark red robes was washing a bright saffron coloured shroud in the river. He dunked it repeatedly and then squeezed out the water or slapped it repeatedly on the rocks in the same manner I had seen Indian women everywhere do their laundry. The difference was he was clearly a European. After five minutes he climbed up to the wall where I was standing and hung the saffron cloth over it to dry. We got talking and he told me he was Swiss but had lived in India for over ten years, just travelling around. His Indian robes and long hair, which was scraped back into a ponytail, gave him the appearance of one who was still travelling the hippy trail and had no intention whatsoever of ever going home. The saffron cloth, he told me, had been the shroud that covered the dead body of the last person to be cremated. Why he had been chosen to receive it he didn't explain. But he told me that he knew lots of people in Varanasi and had lived here for some time. Perhaps they saw him as one of their own. However, a couple of Indian men who approached us clearly didn't. One of them carried a small wicker basket. He flipped open the lid and out slid a cobra, which curled round his wrist and rose up in the classic striking pose. I had already seen a few of these characters with their doctored cobras who make a living giving cheap thrills to tourists. They drew a total blank with us though.

My new-found friend just reached across, took hold of the snake, draped it round his neck, gave it a peck on the top of its head and turned back to our conversation. I just stood there goggle-eyed. The two Indian lads soon got bored with his total lack of reaction, grabbed their prized possession and wandered off, no doubt in search of a more impressionable audience. It was early afternoon and the hot sun didn't take long to dry out the shroud, and so after a few minutes he folded neatly, tucked it under his arm, bade me farewell and left me to watch the cremation.

It was a vividly colourful affair, and a noisy one too. I heard the funeral procession long before I saw it. The ringing of bells and the wailing of chants announced its arrival as a litter appeared from the warren of narrow streets, carried shoulder high by mourners, and started to make its way down the steep steps of the *ghat* towards the river. The body was covered in a gold shroud that looked like baking foil, and garlands of flowers had been strewn across it. The main body of mourners filed behind. The mourners carried the litter past the pyre and down to the edge of the river where the four men scooped up handfuls of the sacred water and anointed the body. A few feet away water buffaloes drank and pissed in the water. Then they carried the litter up to the funeral pyre, and with a crescendo of wailing from the mourners the shroud was removed and the body, swathed in muslin cloth and looking a little like an Egyptian mummy, was laid on the pyre. The cloth blackened in the intense heat almost immediately. Then, ever so slowly, it sank into the funeral pyre's fiery embrace and was consumed. Inquisitive dogs alerted by the sweet smell of scorching flesh were beaten away with sticks by some of the mourners.

"I am seeing you in Mr. Fahim's taxi, many days now," said the man. I cannot remember exactly how I replied but I recall that I had no need to doubt him.

"Are you are knowing," he continued, "that a taxi booked at the hotel reception is carrying forty percent extra charge. And the man working in the hotel, he is being a cousin of Mr. Fahim."

I had to grant him that figured. "When are you leaving for airport?" was his next question. I told him that, in fact, I was travelling to my next destination by train, leaving from Moghulserai station that evening at 6.30pm.

"I am giving you very good price for my taxi," he said, and with that we struck the deal at 250 rupees and I told him to meet me outside the hotel at 5.30pm. According to my Lonely Planet guide Moghulserai station was only twelve kilometres from Varanasi and I figured that an hour would leave me plenty of time to get there.

"You will be being here outside hotel at 5 o'clock please," he replied.

The next leg of my journey was to Darjeeling, and it was going to be the longest train ride thus far. From Varanasi I would be travelling overnight to New Jaipalguri, or NJP as it is more commonly known, one of the major railway terminuses in Northern India. It was a 15 hours overnight train journey and I would arrive at 10.00am the next morning. From there I had to make my way to the bus terminal in the neighbouring town of Siliguri. And from there I would be taking a bus up to Darjeeling, a further journey of six hours. So with all that travelling ahead I thought I would take it easy for the afternoon, relaxing in the gardens of the nearby Suray Hotel. Not knowing what the catering would be like on the train, I took the precaution of stocking up on a big plate of chicken curry and a couple of naans the size of small wagon wheels. The effect of the big meal, a couple of cold beers and the warm sunshine soon had me nodding off when I was roughly shaken awake. It was the taxi driver. He had seen me walk into the hotel hours earlier so he knew where I was, and he was now insisting in no uncertain terms that we get going. I checked my watch and it had barely gone 4.30pm. I was a little disgruntled at this. I had in effect a full night and day's worth of travelling ahead of me and considered every moment in the garden of the hotel

precious. I had allowed an hour to make the twelve kilometres to the
station, which I thought would leave me plenty of time to spare.
Of course, I should have known by then that ordinary rules do not apply
in India, especially when getting anywhere was concerned. Anyway,
the taxi driver wasn't having any of it, which as it turned out was just as
well. Somewhat reluctantly I gathered my things and trudged after him.
Give him his due the man knew his trade. More to the point he knew
his city, and what the traffic would be like at that time of day.

He drove like a maniac. On the way to the station we had to cross over
the main Delhi to Calcutta road. The junction itself was a straightforward
two lanes crossroads, just like you would find on the outskirts of any
English town. The difference was that it handled the volume of heavy
goods traffic you would more normally find on the entire M25. And it
was a total free-for-all. There wasn't even a set of traffic lights. There was
a gesture of sorts towards traffic control in the shape of a small concrete
island in the middle of the junction where a policeman stood blowing
a whistle and waving his arms around wildly. The chances of it being
heard above the combined horn blaring power of several thousand tonnes
of road haulage, coming straight at him from all directions, were remote
to say the least. We did what everybody else did and launched ourselves
into the fray. It was the automotive equivalent of white water rafting.
You set your sights on a point on the opposite bank and struggled like
hell against the current to get there. It wasn't just the traffic crossing in
front of you from both directions you had to look for, the traffic behind
you was quite happy to push you into the oncoming wall of battered
metal without a care. So with much horn blaring, cursing and feet
dancing from accelerator pedal to brake from my driver in the front,
and teeth-clenched praying from me in the back, we bolted across
the intersection.

Having survived that the next challenge was the bridge. It was the only
way out of town, and every cart, rickshaw, motorbike, car, bus, lorry and
taxi got funnelled onto it. The road simply couldn't hold the colossal

volume of traffic, which spilled off on to what passed for the pavement. But there wasn't actually a pavement. What normally would have been the pavement was where people lived in makeshift dwellings, which were little more than tents. It was not uncommon to see anxious mothers grab their meagre prized possessions, which in a couple of cases included their children, and leg it out of the way of auto rickshaws and taxis, as they ploughed their way through what moments earlier had been their living rooms.

We made it to the railway station with ten minutes to spare. But when I walked in and looked at the station clock, I realised I was ten minutes slow. The helpful taxi driver had told me to go to the reservations window and ask there about my train. Panic overtook any English sensibilities and for the first time in my life I ignored the 20 or so people standing there and barged my way to the front of the queue, where I was told to go to platform two. I dashed off to the walkway that spanned the platforms. Wouldn't you know it, platform two was at the far end. I was now beginning to stagger under the weight of my backpack as I ran as best I could. The ramp down to platform two appeared on my right, and the train, well, a train, was standing there. I had no idea whether it was mine or not. It was already bulging at the rivets with passengers and the chai wallahs were still busily engaged in passing cups of their milky brew through the windows to passengers inside. It had to be my train I reasoned. I hobbled along the platform, swerving to avoid the trolleys of the food hawkers, looking for the second class air-conditioned sleeper carriages. I was looking for berth nineteen on sleeper carriage A1. Three sleeper carriages were located in the middle of the train. Mine, I reasoned, had to be the first one in line, and I scrambled aboard. By now, I was the last passenger and everyone else had spread themselves out and established their territories. Not that there was a lot of room to do so in a fully booked sleeper carriage. I made my way down to the middle of the carriage to berth nineteen. The section was occupied by an extended Indian family of three generations and their assorted luggage, which, as well as suitcases, included rolled up carpets and boxes of household appliances. This wonderful array of booty had been painstakingly packed away on my berth. I apologised and waved my piece of paper from the reservations centre in Lucknow in front of their noses that said I had berth nineteen. As luck would have it one of their party, a middle-aged man of about 50, spoke some English. I sat down beside him and chatted while two of his sons started unpacking my berth of all their belongings and re-packed them under other berths, and in a couple of instances, under the bums of a couple of ageing aunts. It took them a good quarter of an hour of hauling, pushing and squeezing to accomplish the task, which I have to say, they completed with the best of grace. They had just completed the job when the train conductor ambled along with his never-to-be-seen-without sheets of computer printout paper. He took one look at my ticket, and told me that I should be in the next carriage. Highly embarrassing. I apologised profusely as the two sons rolled up their sleeves again and contemplated re-packing all the stuff so that it all went back exactly where it had come from in the first place. I left them to it and shuffled off to the next carriage, which turned out to be just as crowded as the one I had left. Curtains were drawn across all the compartments and I popped my head into a couple of wrong ones before I found my correct berth. My cheery "sorries" were met with blank stares. I ended up sharing with a family of four. They had obviously thought they were going to have the compartment to themselves and were not quite able to hide their disappointment when I arrived. The father spoke very good English, but unlike most Indians I had met was reluctant to practise it on me.

The train roused itself as one at about 7.00 the next morning. I lay there giving the family below some space so they could get themselves ready for the day. Chai wallahs had got on at the previous station and were patrolling the corridors rattling their tin cups and carrying large buckets of hot tea, and shouting out "chai, chai". I clambered down from my bunk and went to the toilet at the end of the carriage. A man was standing by the open door of the carriage. Early morning sunlight sparkled on the surface of the water in the rice paddies which skipped by. We were passing through the Patna region. When I returned to my bunk I wished the father *Namaste* and he told me that the train would be arriving at New Jaipalguri one and a half hours late, at about 11 o'clock. I was not complaining, if it had not been running late in the first place, I would not have been on it. I took myself off and sat on the floor by the open doorway for a couple of hours, happy to watch India roll by to the accompaniment of the rhythm of the clackety-clack of the train on the track, and to enjoy being buffeted by a crisp cool breeze.

To be honest, going to Darjeeling was never my idea in the first place. It was Dr Dandapani's suggestion back in Wembley. But I am very glad I took the good doctor's advice. The weather was hot and sunny as I emerged from the station. New Jaipalguri was a large sprawling town with little of cultural interest, and I needed to get to the neighbouring town of Siliguri where my bus left from the Tenzing Norgay Bus Terminal. I flagged down a passing cycle rickshaw and hopped aboard. After a while the rickshaw driver turned off the main road and we went down some side streets that were lined with little shops and stalls. We crossed over a small bridge that spanned the trickle of a brackish, brown river. The water was stagnant, assorted animals rooted at its edges, and I detected the telltale whiff of open sewer. A few hundred yards later we came across a cricket match. I tapped the rickshaw driver on the shoulder and gestured for him to stop so that I could watch. Being Indian he was more than happy to do so, not so much for the rest it afforded him, but because everyone in India shared a passion for the game. He climbed up beside me on the rickshaw seat so that he could get a better view of the game and together we enjoyed a grandstand view over a low wall and onto the pitch. We watched a few overs, discussing the merits of the players with gestures in the international language that only men who are fanatical about sport seem to have mastered, and then after witnessing a period of some pretty ineffectual bowling, we moved off and continued on our way.

Soon afterwards we hit Hillcart Road, the main drag linking the two towns. It was typically congested with all sorts of mechanical and animal drawn traffic and lined with tall buildings. Shops huddled at street level, surmounted by rows of offices, which in turn were surmounted by apartments. It was like the architectural equivalent of a human pyramid of acrobats standing on one another's shoulders. At pavement level the street was a riot of shop signage. Hand-painted signs, printed signs, neon signs, they rubbed shoulders with one another as they silently shouted their wares and jostled for position to catch a passing eye.

At the bus terminal attendants stood at the entrance asking passengers their destination and guiding them to the right bus. It was a blessed relief for once not to have to worry about having a reservation, or rather lack of one, and I bought a one-way ticket to Darjeeling. When I turned round an attendant was there to take me to the right bay where the Darjeeling bus stood waiting. It was an old rickety twenty-four seater. I handed my backpack up to a man on the roof who tied it to the roof rack, securely I hoped. I was one of the first passengers so I settled myself into a corner of the bench seat at the back, hoping that the window I had chosen to sit by would afford me some good views as we climbed our way up into the Himalaya.

My guidebook told me that Darjeeling sprawled across a ridge at seven thousand feet so the bus was going to have to make quite a climb. The bus quickly filled up and my co-passengers were mountain people with the distinctive features I normally associated with people from Nepal and Tibet. I soon found myself wedged into my corner by a crush of people who chatted and jabbered to one another, and seemingly everyone else on the bus, at once. There was a strange sense of excitement as we headed off, a lifting of everyone's spirits. It was like the feeling you get when you set sail on a voyage. But then this was to be no ordinary bus ride. Within half an hour we had left the town behind us and had started to climb. The bus climbed steadily uphill and as soon as we escaped Siliguri the landscape gave way to gently rolling hills covered in tall, evergreen trees. The gradient of the road began to rise in a series of steps and the higher we climbed the more my eye was taken ever upwards to where the distant outline of peaks and ridges could be glimpsed amongst the clouds.

It was a couple of hours into the journey before we caught up with the Toy Train. This is the most famous train in India and runs every day from NJP to Darjeeling, landslides and other Acts of God permitting. From the moment we left the Siliguri we had criss-crossed over its tracks for mile after mile. We heard it well before we saw it. Its shrill whistle echoed back to us at intervals as we slowly gained on it. The train's proper name is the Darjeeling and Himalayan Railway, but throughout the subcontinent and to railway enthusiasts the world over, it's known simply as the Toy Train, and for very good reason. My first sighting of it was a flash of bright blue through the trees shrouded in cotton wool puffs of white smoke.

It's impossible to describe the Toy Train without recourse to the language of the nursery because it is a real-life version of every illustration you have ever seen in a Thomas the Tank Engine storybook. This became even more apparent when we caught up with it a few minutes later. The road and the rails ran parallel for most of the climb up to Darjeeling and only separated and went their separate ways when the terrain dictated, before they came together at a later point, and ran side by side again. At times this gave the road route a march over the train, and at others it allowed the train to steam ahead of us. The unwritten rule seemed to be that the venerable old Toy Train always had right of way. The second time I saw the train it emerged from the trees to my right with an angry blast of its whistle that said "coming through". The locomotive was painted the brightest blue and was not much bigger than a large commercial van. It had all the features you would expect of a toy train, a round clock face up front, two bulging lamps for eyes, a squat chimney stack that belched puffballs of white smoke, a barrel-bellied boiler, big black mudguards and a proud engine driver standing on the footplate. Behind it, the train pulled a small coal wagon, and behind that two passenger cars and a luggage car.

Over the next half hour our paths crossed half a dozen times, and we always seemed to arrive just ahead of the train. Just as we approached a point where the road crossed over the tracks we would hear a shrill blast of its whistle and the little train would appear from out of the trees, angrily huffing, and puffing, and chuffing its way through like an old lady at a rummage sale who is determined to get to the bargains first. We would politely stop and watch the train as it chugged forward relentlessly right across our nose, then as soon as it had passed, the bus driver would gun the engine and try and beat it to the next intersection. We played cat and mouse with the Toy Train like this as both the train and the bus climbed for mile after mile high into the foothills of the mountain range. Sometimes we would hear its whistle only faintly and would think we had it beat at last, only for the road to take a wide course round an outcrop and allow the train time to catch up so that at the next point where the road crossed the rails our driver would have to jump on the brakes right at the last minute, as with another shrill blast the Toy Train came bustling out of the trees all steam, whistle and determination to be first. However, the brave little train was always on something of a loser.

It generally takes anything between eight to ten hours for the Toy Train to make the climb to Darjeeling so the bus was always going to be quicker. Finally we pulled ahead of it and knew we would not see it again until it arrived in Darjeeling. As we climbed away I continued to hear whistle echoing through the hills. Angrier than before, it shouted after us, "come back here you bastards, I'll get you in the end".

There were any number of villages and small towns dotted along the route, and by the time we had gone half way our bus was packed to the gills with what must have been up to sixty people. The two-seater benches were now accommodating three and there was not a spare patch of standing room to be had. There were three means of transport up and down from Darjeeling. As well as the Toy Train and the bus service there were also shared jeeps. Basically, you sat in a jeep in Siliguri or Darjeeling and waited for it to fill up with six or seven other passengers, and when it did you were off. The shared jeeps were the quickest way up and down beating the buses by on average a couple of hours per journey. Every means of transport was a lifeline for the towns and villages though and we dropped off numerous packages of food, household items and other bits and pieces. However, there was one other unofficial means of transport that only worked in one direction – down. The villagers made excellent use of the rails of the Toy Train by making little railway toboggans which were made by bolting sets of wheels onto flat pieces of wood. To one of the sets of wheels they would attach a crude brake-lever affair. Then they simply plonked their little railway toboggans on the rails, sat down on the wooden platform, lifted up their heels and they were away. It was a very cheap way of getting down to the next village, and in theory you could have gone all the way from Darjeeling to the outskirts of Siliguri on one of these things. Of course, it only worked in one direction, so they had to get the bus back, but at least it saved them half a fare. I lost count of the number of children, mums and dads and even grandparents who zipped past me on these things. Whenever I did they always had huge grins plastered all over their faces. If I could have commuted to work like that every day, I thought, office life wouldn't have been so bad.

Eventually, as we climbed higher, the trees gave way to the tea plantations that make Darjeeling famous. A carpet of knee-high green bushes cloaked the undulating landscape in all directions looking like a sea of broccoli. It grew steadily colder and mistier as we climbed above the clouds and then, without warning, we were there. The road circled round a steep bend and ahead of us I saw Darjeeling clinging by its fingertips to a long ridge a few miles distant.

As soon as we hit the narrow street that led into the town we rejoined the railway tracks of the Toy Train. There was no room for a separate railway line so they built it down the middle of the high street. Twice a day the little trains puff their way through the pedestrians and past the shops on their way in and out of the station. The bus dropped us off in the market square where all the buses, jeeps and taxis congregated. It was flanked on both side by rows of the smarter shops, bars and kiosks, and behind it sprawled an open-air market. It was early evening and stepping off the bus the cold quickly began to seep into my bones. I wasted no time in grabbing a taxi as I was keen to find somewhere to stay. I had picked out the New Elgin from my Lonely Planet and five minutes later the taxi drew up outside the hotel.

The New Elgin was a throwback to the days of the Raj, when armies of civil servants from Delhi would escape the fierce summer of Rajasthan and decamp lock stock and administrative barrel to the hill stations. Most hotels nowadays are luxurious, efficient and totally forgettable. Not so the New Elgin. Architecturally it was low-rise and seemed to tumble down the ridge on which it perched in a series of layered steps. It overlooked the town of Darjeeling and the view beyond stretched out over the tea plantations to distant mountains beyond. Its roof and walls were a greyish green, which meant that it blended in with the dark green coniferous trees that surrounded it, and the low angle, pitched roofs helped to meld it into the surrounding terrain. I stepped into the reception and was enveloped by a cuddle of warmth that came from a cast iron, wood-burning stove that stood in the corner. Who needs a greeter when you've got one of those. It was only half a dozen paces to the reception desk and on two of them the floorboards gave me a welcoming, homely squeak. A glance to my right revealed a small sitting room with upholstered sofas and chairs whose needlepoint had seen better days, but which added faded charm to the place. They were arranged around a coal fire that crackled loudly in the grate inside a grand looking marble fireplace. Prints of English hunting scenes hung on the walls, and on a wall-mounted plinth stood a scale model of H.M.S. Victory, which had obviously been a hand crafted labour of love on someone's part, perhaps painstakingly pieced together, piece by piece, by a retired military attaché many years ago.

I negotiated a room for a couple of nights and was invited to sit in the drawing room while they prepared it for me. I collapsed into an armchair and noticed that the only other occupant of the drawing room was a small bundle of white fur stretched out in front of the fire hogging its warmth. From beneath a floppy white fringe, two beady black eyes that looked like small lumps of coal surveyed me suspiciously. Some London and New York hotels boast a writer in residence. The New Elgin had Dax, a Tibetan Terrier, and every passing maid, porter and waiter stopped to give him a scratch behind the ear or a tummy rub. Dax was obviously of the opinion that such adulation was no more than his rightful due, and if anyone dared to walk by without affording him a pat or a stroke, he would give out a muffled little bark of disgust.

My room was dominated by a huge mahogany bedstead with antique furniture and other old world bric-a-brac. A steaming hot bath was the ultimate luxury after a long haul on an overnight train and hours on the bus all the way up from Siliguri. Then, after a meal in the hotel's restaurant, I was delighted to discover the New Elgin's defining feature. While I relaxed in the lounge, paying court to Dax while sipping a large brandy, a maid had been in my room and put a hot water bottle in my bed. I slipped between the thick, cotton sheets, pulled up the heavy covers, and slept like the proverbial baby.

I am not what you might call a dedicated hill walker but I have been known to enjoy the odd tramp over the Yorkshire moors when visiting friends, so long as there has been the prospect of a decent pub lunch at the end of it. I have even been known to walk up the occasional escalator rather than ride it all the way to the top. Hardly the credentials to equip one for a visit to the Himalayan Mountain Institute I grant you, and I still don't know the difference between a *coll* and a *couloir*. So why did I go? Because it was there I suppose.

The place lay further along the ridge from Darjeeling, a good twenty minutes walk along some pretty steep roads, so my first thought was to whistle up a taxi. But then some sort of sense of occasion kicked in and I thought that the prospect of turning up at this monument to mountaineering in a car would be insulting to say the least. So in honour of all those intrepid climbers the Institute celebrated I felt the very least I could do was walk there. It took me all of half an hour and due to the altitude I arrived gasping and wheezing.

It turned out to be not so much a museum as it was a shrine to those brave men and women who had pitted themselves against one of the most daunting of physical and mental challenges known to man, the ascent of Everest. I learnt that the Institute's Director for many years before his death was Darjeeling's most famous son, Tenzing Norgay. In many cases these climbers had endured unimaginable hardships and lived to tell the tale. And in some others they had not. All the successful ascents were featured and their stories were told simply with photographs, text panels, notes from personal diaries, memorabilia and pieces of equipment, which were revered by the more knowledgeable almost as sacred relics. You didn't have to know anything about mountaineering for the place to sweep you up like an avalanche. The strongest impression it made on me was the courage, strength and incredible levels of human endurance these people must have possessed to go in pursuit of their dreams. As every schoolboy and Trivial Pursuit enthusiast can tell you Everest was first conquered by Sir Edmund Hillary in 1953. Since then we've had the development of satellite weather forecasting and direction finding, a revolution in lightweight cold resistant clothing that owes much to space walks, another revolution in what we know about diet and nutrition in extreme conditions, rapid advances in mountaineering equipment and the advent of corporate sponsorship, whereby companies are happy to hand over millions to pay for all this stuff in order to get their names in on the act. Back in the fifties it wasn't just a question of climbing Everest, first you had to get to the foot of the mountain by hoofing it across the rest of the Himalaya in the first place. They had to trek their way in before they went up, and in all probability wearing gear and equipment today's average fell walker wouldn't be seen dead in, "dead" being the operative word probably.

If Hillary's famous ascent wasn't impressive enough, I then learnt about Mallory's ill-fated attempt in 1924. Many years after Hillary his frozen remains were discovered only a few hundred feet from the summit, giving rise to one of the most hotly debated questions in mountaineering history. Was he on his way up, or down, when he slipped and died? Had Mallory beaten Hillary to the summit nearly 30 years earlier? Chances are we will never know, and thousands of copies of pub quiz books won't have to be recalled for a bit of urgent re-printing.

Inspired by these feats of daring-do, that afternoon I too set myself my own high altitude, personal challenge, to have tea at the Windamere Hotel. After all, standing at the very top of Darjeeling, I can assure you that high tea doesn't get much higher than when it's taken at the Windamere. Fortunately, the Windamere was only a five minutes walk from the New Elgin, be it a steep one.

From the terrace of the hotel, which stood on one of the highest ridges in Darjeeling, I looked out over the majestic Himalaya towards a distant Everest.

The view was dominated in the foreground by the massive lump that is Kanchenjunga, the third highest mountain in the world.

Tea took place in a cosy little snug called Bearspark Parlour, which featured the same faded furniture that gave the New Elgin its Raj relic charm. A fire burned in a brick fireplace. Old dusty hardback books and an assortment of prints and photos lined the walls. All except for one wall which was given over to a large painting entitled, The Spirit of the Toy Train. It was an impressionistic work and showed the famous little train rounding a particularly steep curve in the forest and exhaling billowing clouds of steam. I could almost hear its shrill whistle.

The only other occupants of the cosy little parlour were a crusty looking English professor type who was waxing lyrical about icons in English literature to a young and very pretty looking girl of undergraduate age. I hovered in their vicinity in the hope that they might acknowledge me and allow me to join in the conversation, but he was not having any of it. Instead, I read the walls. They were lined with newspaper cuttings and articles about the hotel and some of the ascents of Kanchenjunga and Everest made by some of the hotel's more intrepid residents.

Tea, when it arrived, came on a silver tray. There were cheese and tomato sandwiches, cut into neat little triangles and with the crusts cut off. They were accompanied by a plate of crunchy biscuits and a couple of slices of banana cake. I had to admit I was a little disappointed not to see anything bun like, dotted with currants, toasted and dripping in butter, or any bowls of jam and clotted cream. The tea itself was pale in colour, delicately scented and served with warm milk and sugar to taste. Just a drop of milk was enough to turn the brew cloudy. I picked up my saucer and turned it over and there on the base was the Windamere's own crest and the name Hitkari Potteries of India. The clinking of silverware and crockery mingled with the crackling that emanated from the grate, and the sooty smell of burning coal wafted across the room. As the heat from the fire began to soak in, I imagined how easy it must have been for high tea at the Windamere to make all those officers and administrators of the Raj feel quite homesick. The Residency in Lucknow had shown me that the English are unsurpassed at turning far flung parts of the world into pockets of little England, and I suspect that the Victorians in particular were past masters of the trick. No other nation manages to pull it off quite so authentically. So, as I relaxed in the glow of the fire and listened to the sedate tick-tock of the grandfather clock in the corner, it was easy to imagine that outside the door stretched the Chilterns in shades of autumn gold, or the rolling hills of the Sussex Downs.

I left Darjeeling in a shared jeep. Dozens of them were lined up in the market square waiting for passengers to make up a full complement, which took six people. I was the first aboard and it took just under an hour for another five passengers to join me. By being first I had bagged a seat at the back which looked out backwards, affording me an uninterrupted view all the way down, a journey which took about four hours.

At NJP station I had the platform almost to myself while I waited for the connecting train to take me to Calcutta's Sealdah station. For once, there was no problem with my reserved berth and I shared an overnight journey with a charming Indian businessman. Emerging from Sealdah station I had a day to kill in Calcutta before I took the Bubhaneshwar Express to New Delhi, which left at five o'clock that evening from Howrah station and which lay on the other side of the Hooghly river. I decided to go to Howrah station first, dump my backpack in the left-luggage room, and be free to explore what I could of Calcutta in the few hours that I had in the city. Stepping off the train I was immediately pounced on by a rickshaw *wallah*. In Calcutta, it seems, they don't wait for you to emerge from the station, they prey on you on the platforms. I told him I wanted to go to Howrah station and we negotiated a fare of forty rupees, but the smallest denomination I had was a one hundred rupees note. There was no way in the world he was going to have change, so I explained the situation to him as simply as I could. In a flash he grabbed the note out of my hand, and just as I thought he was about to do a runner he dived into the crowd beckoning me to follow him. He fought his way through the pack, with me following in his slipstream, over to a newspaper seller who was sitting in the dirt surrounded by a sea of papers and magazines. My guy handed over my one hundred rupees note and got a fifty rupees note and five tens in return, which he handed to me in cupped hands and with a little bow. Shame on me for doubting him. We made our way out of the station and into the bright sunshine where the teeming street life of Calcutta smacked me in the face. There were no preliminaries. Calcutta is a straight-in-at-the-deep-end kind of city. We emerged into a forest of rickshaw staves, hundreds of them which poked up into the air like a bristling porcupine's back. In amongst the rickshaws were dotted little clearings where food stalls doled out dahl, and tobacco sellers sold little plugs of chewing tobacco that were wrapped in silver foil or a palm leaf. Beggars by the score and dusty sadhus, in skimpy ragged loincloths or wearing nothing at all, stretched out under tattered awnings.

My rickshaw wallah was perhaps a couple of inches over five feet tall and he could not have weighed an ounce over six stone. Back home he'd have been thrown out of jockey school for not being beefy enough. He wore a blue shirt that had never seen a spin cycle in its life and a grubby dhoti that was wrapped round his waist and fell to just below his knees to reveal spindle like shins. He was also barefoot. At first I felt very uncomfortable about being in a man drawn rickshaw, being pulled along by a barefoot runner. But if there was any indignity involved it was totally at my expense. Sitting, perched, high up on what was basically an open cart, I soon felt completely ridiculous. I tried to console myself with the knowledge that thousands of Indians in Calcutta use these rickshaws every day to go to work, attend school, to do the shopping, or generally go about their business. And for many rickshaw wallahs the work was a vital lifeline. However, as we eased into the early morning commuter traffic I couldn't help but feel that every passer-by was staring at me thinking there goes an another bloody stupid looking Englishman who still thinks he's some kind of Sahib. The women who looked at me lifted their veils to cover the lower part of their faces, not out of modesty as per usual I was convinced, but to hide their smirking.

But any thoughts of embarrassment melted away as soon as I realised that a traditional rickshaw can take you places, and show you things, you wouldn't experience otherwise. We turned into a narrow backstreet which was no more than a few feet wide. Shopkeepers had set up shop in doorways selling batteries, old tape recorders, pots and pans and various other household appliances. Tailors hunched over rickety old sewing machines which they pedalled with their feet as they mended old suit jackets. And food hawkers fried morsels in pans of smoking mustard oil that scented the air with a heady tang. Wherever there were a few square feet, someone had set up shop or was doing business from it.

The backstreets were an unseen hive of work and activity, which attracted thousands of shoppers who crammed into the narrow confines. People squeezed up against the walls as we passed by, turning sideways onto us so to avoid the rickshaw's large wagon wheels. In the space of only a few yards we went from a narrow back street, lined with tall buildings that created an avenue of shade, into an open square which was blasted by the heat of the early morning sun and where huge piles of the city's rubbish rotted and festered. Then we disappeared again back into the warren of narrow streets. Looking left and right as the rickshaw wallah's bare feet pat-patted along the shady alleyways at a constant rhythm, I caught glimpses of dark, smoky courtyards where old men in turbans sat and talked, or children played at their mothers' feet as they cooked or sewed. Then, like a light switch being flicked, we emerged into the full glare of a wide, major road junction at the height of the morning rush hour. Twelve lanes of nose to tail traffic revved angrily at red lights. A few seconds later the lights changed and my rickshaw wallah made a desperate lunge to cross the junction before we got swallowed up in a tsunami of moving metal. We dashed across the intersection with only seconds to spare, and disappeared back into the warren of narrow back streets like a rabbit escaping a pack of hounds down a bolt hole. In the distance

I kept glimpsing a monstrous construction of grey metal that dominated the skyline, a huge, shapeless trellis of steel struts, like Gormenghast fashioned out of Meccano. "Howrah Bridge, Sah," he shouted at me over his shoulder. The bridge spanned the River Hooghly in one long step without getting its concrete feet wet. As we arrived at the foot of the bridge my rickshaw wallah suddenly pulled up short like a steeplechaser balking at Becher's Brook in the Grand National. Rickshaws were not allowed on the bridge, so the only option was Shanks's pony. I paid off the rickshaw wallah and he helped me set my backpack on my shoulders before giving me a cheery farewell, and with that I set off across the bridge on foot.

The Howrah Bridge is one of the main thoroughfares into Calcutta, and at that time of the morning it thronged with thousands of pedestrians heading into the city. The trouble was I was heading out, so it was a case of a solitary thirteen stone Englishman, with backpack, against a human tsunami of Indian workers and commuters who were all late for work. Head down, I formed a one man flying wedge and aimed for the dead centre of the oncoming rush, in the vain hope it would part for me like the Red Sea once I had built up a sufficient head of steam. Fat chance. It took me the best part of half an hour to struggle across the Howrah Bridge, a distance of no more than a few hundred yards. I made it to the other side battered, bruised, sweating profusely; hoarse from shouting, okay, let's make that screaming expletives at the top of my lungs, but otherwise intact.

At the station I checked the departures board for the time of the Bubhaneshwar Express, which was to take me on the final leg of my Indian journey to Delhi. The train was already alongside the platform so I made my way down looking for the Second Class Air-Conditioned Sleeper Carriage number two, where, as far as I was concerned, I had a berth reserved. Some thoughtful soul had scribbled A2 next to the door of one of the sleeper carriages, and next to it they had selloptaped another list of passenger names. With a sense of ridiculous optimism I scanned it anyway, and Wow! There it was, my name, and next to it berth number

17. For once, it was not one in a group of four, but was one of a set of two on the other side of the corridor. Number 17 was the bottom bunk which meant I had a double window view all to myself. I settled in looking forward to watching India trundle by outside the window. Half an hour after the train pulled out of the station the conductor came along, checked my ticket and promptly ticked my name off his list, without any more than a polite thank you. We crawled out of the station and snaked our way through the shoulder-to-shoulder suburbs, which eventually gave way to fields and villages surrounded by waterlogged rice fields. In amongst them stood palm trees with large fronds that flopped like slouch hats and created welcome pockets of shade for people and their animals. Small children drove herds of oxen, beating the more lazy ones with bamboo sticks. Clouds of dust lifted off their rumps into the air with each thwack, like dirt being beaten from a carpet.

There is something undeniably magical about watching a landscape go by through the window of a train. Framed by the window, it was like watching the world's longest panning shot, accompanied by a rhythmic, but now pleasantly familiar, clackety-clack soundtrack. Then, just when I thought things couldn't get any better, they did. A train steward appeared with a tray covered by a cloth and placed it on the bunk beside me. "Please," he said, gesturing towards it. I lifted the cloth and there was a *thali*, a complete meal consisting of dollops of steamed rice, mixed vegetables, dahl, lamb curry and a scrawny chicken leg. I surveyed it with a wary eye, but my nose was urging me to plunge in regardless, and for once I let hunger overcome common sense, picked up the tin fork it came with, and tentatively speared a small mouthful of the curry.

"You will be all right, it's quite safe," said the passenger sitting opposite me on the other side of the carriage. He was a middleaged Indian gentleman who was dressed in a dark suit and tie. He was slightly balding and his hair was tinged with silver-grey. When he spoke it was with a quiet authority. "When they know how many passengers they have on board, they phone the station down the line where the food is cooked fresh. It hasn't been reheated."

He turned out to be an accountant who worked for Indrail and I told him that I had enjoyed my time travelling by train immensely. "Oh, I am so glad," he said, and then proceeded to give me a long, but fascinating lecture about the history and extent of it. He bombarded me with a blizzard of statistics which he reeled off the top of his head. "Indrail is the largest employer in the world you know, we have 1.6 million employees. In fact, it is reckoned that over eighty million people depend on it for their living in one way or another. And two million people are using it every day."

The last time I had heard such a machine gun fire delivery of facts and figures about Indian Railways had been in Wembley, and I wondered if by some remote possibility he was actually related to Dr. Dandapandi.

"And do you know that in Mumbai on one particular commuter line two thousand people lose their lives under the wheels of trains every year," he continued. "We have 38,000 level crossings and 100,000 bridges to maintain, which is a lot of work but fortunately in India labour is very cheap."

He was generous in his praise for the British Raj for bringing the railways to India in the first place, either that I thought or he was just being polite. And if so then this would not have surprised me. The odd train conductor aside, I had encountered nothing but consideration and politeness from my fellow passengers on all my train journeys, and no little generosity of spirit and a lot of patience and understanding besides. Spending nights travelling on these trains had been like being invited to stay with Indian families in their homes, or being invited to spend the night in an Indian village as the guest of honour. Whoever had advised Gandhi to get to know India by travelling around it by train had given the Mahatma excellent advice. My new travelling companion justly had a lot to be proud of, but it had little to do with the scale of the infrastructure.

THREE

The Oldest Backpacker in Town

If there is one address that sums up all the escape, romance and adventure of backpacker travel, it's Bangkok's Khao San Road, the backpacker capital of the world. Not bad for a crowded street lined with cheap B&Bs and bars, where young Australians, French, Germans, Americans and other Wanderlusters from all over the world congregated and swapped adventure stories that hailed from Nepal to New Zealand. For years the Khao San Road had been a cultural crossroads for every new-ager, faded hippy, and twenty- first century drop-out who had simply had enough and George Bailey-like had set off to see the world and discover a little about themselves in the process. Then its fame went mainstream with the publication of *The Beach*, the international bestseller which was later turned into a Hollywood smash starring Leonardo Dicaprio. Even I knew enough to know that the Khao San Road occupied almost mythical status amongst the Lonely Planet reading classes. So it came as something of a surprise when my taxi dropped me off outside a branch of Boots. Apparently, Nottingham's most famous retailer had also beaten a path to this far-flung outpost of South East Asia, which to my mind didn't exactly chime with what the experience was supposed to be all about. But handy if one ran out of toilet paper or needed a new toothbrush whenever things got a little bit too intrepid for comfort.

I went off in search of a room determined to bunk down in a typical backpacker hostel. I popped into more than a dozen B&Bs but the story was always the same, no room at the inn. I was beginning to think that

I would have to look further afield when my luck changed. At the end of the street I came across a small guesthouse that was painted bright green. I pushed open the rickety door and stepped into a small reception area. Two Thai women were sitting behind a wooden counter frying noodles on a gas ring. In the corner a cardboard box housed a wriggling lump that on closer inspection turned out to be six puppies who were barely a couple of weeks old, and to my left stood a rack of pigeonholes where residents had deposited their shoes. I enquired after a room and one of the women led me up a flight of stairs. We climbed past three landings, which were all identical and narrow and housed washing basins and shower cubicles. On reaching the third floor she led me to one of the rooms, opened the door with a key, and ushered me inside.

"Room, 400 baht," she said in lilting, sing-song English. To give the woman her due there was no way she could have been prosecuted under the Trades Descriptions Act, because when she said that for 400 baht you got a room, the room was pretty much all you got. Aside from the ceiling, roof and four walls, the only thing that came with it was a bed and a bare light bulb that hung from the ceiling. There are certain boutique hotels in certain parts of Manhattan and Kensington where minimalism is all the design rage, but this was the real thing, and it didn't cost you a small mortgage payment to spend the night here. It was the sort of place that would have given a Feng Shui master a fit of the screaming abdabs. There was nothing to rearrange. The more I thought about it, the better the prospect got. I wouldn't spend a fortune making long distance international phone calls from my bedside phone, because there wasn't one. I wouldn't get all hot and bothered having to harangue the management about the poor satellite reception on the colour TV because there was no colour TV. And, best of all, when I checked out I wouldn't for once get into one of those annoying arguments about the unaccounted for packet of cashew nuts from the mini bar because the room came *sans* mini bar. I handed over the cash for three nights, threw my rucksack into a corner and myself onto the bed.

It was already dark outside when I awoke. I lay on the bed listening to the beguiling sounds of the bustling city outside. Fifteen minutes later I was showered, changed and on the street. Crowds of cool people sat outside neon lit bars from which rock music reverberated into the night. I strolled past the tables and chairs that spilled off the pavement and on to the road, past the street hawkers frying chicken and pork satay on sticks, and banana fritters that sizzled in aromatic oil. Motorbikes and scooters weaved in and out of the *tuk tuks* that buzzed around in swarms. A table became free and I dived for it. I ordered a Singha beer and started to people watch. It only took me a matter of moments to work out that if you wanted to look cool on the Khao San Road there was a set way to do it.

The first thing I noticed was that for all its freewheeling, devil may care backpacker lifestyle, everyone adhered to a strict dress code. Starting from the bottom and working up, I was surprised to note that flip-flops were surprisingly out. The fashion conscious trendy backpacker wouldn't dare to be seen in anything so blatantly non-ethnic. They all wore leather, open sandals. Patched cut-off jeans, or wraparound sarongs, were the order of the day, and the more colourful the better. T-shirts tended to be plain and faded, and never sported anything as uncool as a western brand name or logo, nor did they ever appear to have been washed on any day with a y in it. Hair was worn straggly and unkempt, loose for women and tied up in short ponytails, with either a piece of string or a rubber band, if you were a bloke. If your hair didn't stretch that far then chances were heads were shaven. Baggy pants and sarongs ended at a minimum mid-calf, although just below the knee seemed to be preferable. And the tops were all ill-fitting so as to reveal a six inch band of honey golden, tanned midriff. The more darkened the strip of torso the more world-weary one could appear, as if chilling out in South East Asia was not just a passing phase but had actually become a way of life. Watches had been replaced with leather bands, and imitation henna tattoos could be bought at street stalls all along the Khao San Road for a few baht. I can't say

I blended in seamlessly and took this all in as I sat there in my bright pink polo shirt, neatly ironed cream chinos and blue yachting shoes with white piping, which I had bought specially at Marks and Spencer and came from something with a name like the "Totally Tropical" collection.

The next couple of days were spent mooching. Great word that, it actually means to wander aimlessly or loiter, and there can be no finer pleasure when visiting a foreign capital for the first time. I wandered around the Royal Palace, a huge compound covering a number of acres. The pavilions and brightly coloured domed temples glistened in the sunlight and surprised me by somehow managing not to appear gaudy. There was no avoiding the crowds and organised tours so I just let myself be swept along with the rest of them. However, later going with the flow took on a completely different meaning. What could be more relaxing, I thought, than a riverboat cruise. I strolled down to the river's edge where there was a ferry stop. The landing was a large wooden construction that was built out into the river on wooden stilts. All manner of boats were tied up and were disgorging cargoes of passengers. The ferries were doing a brisk business and so too were the tourist boats taking small groups or even couples off to the *klongs*, the floating markets that clogged up the backwaters.

"You want long-tail boat?" said a voice and I turned to see a smallish Thai man behind me. He wore flip-flops, cut-off shorts and a faded t-shirt but on his head he sported a yachting cap which he no doubt assumed gave him an air of nautical authority. "We go klongs, two hours, 200 baht," he said giving me a toothy grin.

He led me away from the main pier and we clambered over and through a warren of bamboo poles that had been driven into the ground close to the water's edge and were the piles that supported the ferry terminal overhead to where a cluster of long-tail boats rocked in unison on the wakes of the larger ferry boats crossing the river. They all looked identical to me at first but on closer inspection I saw that no two were the same. They were all made out of so many bits, although having said that they all conformed to the same basic design. They looked like gondolas, except stretched out to about five times a gondola's length, and at least a third of the boat's length was taken up with the engine. Any engine would do it seemed just so long as it had come from nothing smaller than a combine harvester or a Sherman tank. Attached to the engines were 12 feet long poles that ended in propellers, which gave these distinctive water craft their curious name. We clambered aboard and as I took my seat roughly in the middle of the boat I wondered that this was a hell of a lot of boat for one tourist, and recalled photos I'd seen in a National Geographic magazine of one of those Japanese super-tankers where the captain has to get his bike out when he leaves the bridge to go and have a word with the first mate up at the sharp end.

The roar of the engine as it exploded into life was thunderous. The boatman revved it up, clunked the engine into gear, let out the clutch and lowered the propeller at the end of its fishing rod into the water. As the whirring blades, driven eighty horsepower, bit into the still water the stern of the boat dropped a couple of feet into a frothing swirl of angry white water, the bow rose like a rearing stallion and we shot off up the river with me pulling sufficient G to make my face go all wobbly. What I remember of the waterborne sights of the city remains something of a blur. My lasting impression is of fellow river users paddling like crazy to get out of our way. And if we didn't get them there was every chance that our two feet high bow wave would. I gave up trying to look apologetic as we powered past them. They generally responded with a torrent of Thai which I only caught snippets of as they bobbed in and out of sight in the waves of our wake, while they fought gallantly to keep their boats upright.

When I was in Seville once I went to see a bullfight, so clearly I have no shame. The girlie bars of Bangkok are concentrated in and around two streets, Patpong I and Patpong II, which make them sound like a Hollywood skin flick and its sequel. The main Patpong Road was crowded. Neon lit bars lined both sides of the street that straddled a central spine that was made up of market stalls selling all kinds of tourist tat. This turned out to be quite useful. I stood at a stall pretending to inspect a carved wooden elephant but really looking beyond it to scope out the girlie bars. The entrances were adorned with photos of young, nubile Thai girls in various states of undress, and poses that would have brought tears to the eye of the most supple of contortionists. By the entrances stood small groups of hatchet faced, Thai men in black shirts and white silk ties who beckoned at the passing tourists. From their leather jackets some of them surreptitiously produced photographs depicting the dubious delights that lay beyond.

"One hundred baht," said the old woman who manned the stall as she grabbed my hand which was holding the elephant, and waved it under my nose. Feeling like I'd been caught in the act I promptly handed over the cash without even thinking to haggle, grabbed my elephant and left. The trick was going to be to successfully window shop the bars from the relative sanctuary of the street market without acquiring a couple of kilos of tourist tat.

I am always amused to read in the Sunday tabloids that line which always appears at the end of a story exposing "a sleazy sauna on the corner" or similar dodgy massage parlour. Just as the intrepid tabloid hack is about to get more than his collar felt he exits with the sanctimonious editorial line – "at which point our reporter made his excuses and left." Standing outside an establishment unimaginatively called the Pink Pussycat Club, I made my excuses to myself, and apologies to George who I'd imagine wouldn't have been seen dead in such a place, and went in.

I climbed a flight of dimly lit stairs which opened onto a large bar on the first floor overlooking the street. Booths lined the walls and there was a small dance floor, but the main feature of the room was a bar and stage rolled into one that occupied the centre of the room. I took a seat at the bar and ordered a cold Singha beer. In Bangkok the girlie bars may be fleshpots but make no mistake it's the male tourists who are the fresh meat. I hadn't had time to take my first sip before the first scantily dressed girl approached me and asked me to buy her a drink. The proposition was immediately followed by her suggestion that we might spend half an hour together upstairs in private. However, the only thing they got out of me which was firm was a refusal. I politely declined the offer which she took in good grace with a pleasant smile and small shrug of the shoulders. Half a dozen other girls similarly approached me in as many minutes, and as I saw other single men arrive in the bar I watched as the girls descended on them like sharks in a tank when fresh carcasses have been thrown in. When I wasn't busy brushing off bar girls I busied myself watching the cabaret. This was played out on the large stage behind the bar and consisted of two naked Thai girls gyrating their hips on the floor and doing things that involved a bucket of ping-pong balls and a basket ball hoop nailed on to the wall, and all to the strains, and I use the word advisedly, of Jane Birkin singing *Je t'aime*.

The next bar was even more depressing in a cattle market sort of way. Once again the central feature of the room was a raised stage surrounded by a bar. Thai girls, and I mean "girls" because I would hate to guess how young some of them were, danced around stainless steel poles wearing bikinis and with individually numbered discs like bracelets on their wrists. They all wore the same sad, bored yet expectant look and they all moved with the same gyrating hip swivel dance. The music changed every couple of minutes, and each time it changed the girls all took a step to the right and continued dancing at the next pole. This meant that a new girl was added to the line-up each time and the girl who had made it to the end disappeared off stage, and in this way the production line of young flesh was constantly being refreshed. However, not all the girls made it to disappear behind the curtain at the far end of the stage.

This was where the numbered tags they wore on their wrists came into play. When one of them took a punter's fancy he would go to the bar where a line of very smartly dressed middleaged women were sitting behind cash registers. They wore matching uniforms and wouldn't have looked out of place at a suburban supermarket. Men ordered the girls they wanted simply by telling the cash register women their numbers and handed over their money. The woman at the cash register would then repeat the number into a microphone, her tinny sing-song voice echoing above the din of the driving disco music. Then the girl whose number had been announced would step out of the line, come over to the cash register, and take the punter by the hand and disappear with him up a flight of stairs next to the stage. Not all the clientele were serious sex tourists though. I was surprised to see groups of European women taking it all in. Not to mention a noticeable sprinkling of Qantas flight crew.

"I'm staying at the City Residents Apartments," said Steve, his voice crackling over the public payphone I was using in the guesthouse reception. "It's near Patpongs one and two," he added, as if that meant anything to me.

Steve was a producer I had worked with back in London and we had made a number of TV commercials together. He had gone freelance a couple of years beforehand, leaving the heady world of glamorous advertising behind to concentrate on making commercials for veruca ointments and kettle descalers and the like. But it bought him a lot of time to swan around South East Centre going from one dive site to another. A keen scuba diver, I was keen to catch up with Steve as I was determined to learn to scuba dive when I left Bangkok for the island of Koh Samui in a few days time. I wanted to pick his brains. "Just get a cab," said Steve "it should take you less than half an hour."

Cars are for wimps, I said to myself, as I hit the street. There was only one way for a real backpacker to get about Bangkok, and that was by *tuk tuk*. Earlier, I had spent hours buzzing round Bangkok in various tuk-tuks ticking off the tourist sites. I'd discovered that there was simply no better way to get around an Asian city like Bangkok than by these fun little conveyances. Being open air means you are immediately so much closer to the city. And the distinctive, rapid-fire cough of a tuk-tuk's two-stroke engine immediately tells you that you are about to explore a teeming city and that the promise of exotic sights and sounds lies around every corner. One of the things I had learnt about tuk-tuks in Bangkok was that there was never any guarantee of ending up where you had planned to go. No matter how well I rehearsed the Thai name of my destination, to the Thai ear it always came out as something totally different. It went like this. I thought I had asked for the equivalent of Piccadilly Circus and my tuk-tuk driver would smile broadly at me and reply in Thai with something along the lines of, "Ah yes, Balls Pond Road, very cheap, hop in." This hadn't really bothered me. So what if I had ended up somewhere else. It was always interesting and had something to offer. And even though each little journey had taken me two or three stabs to get right, it meant I had seen even more of this fascinating city at close quarters. However, tonight I was armed, I had scribbled down the address of where Steve was staying on a scrap of paper and got a friendly bar girl to write it out in Thai for me. The theory being that I could then wave it under the nose of any passing tuk-tuk driver with a fair degree of certainty that he would then know where I needed to go.

My first impressions were actually rather encouraging. I flagged down a tuk-tuk driver who actually managed to pronounce the words City Residents from the translation. I therefore presumed that he had got the rest of the address straight off the bat as well. We haggled a bit before we agreed a fare of 250 baht and all without a hint of a "Don't know about that guv, I'm not going south of the Chao Phraya River at this time of night." Luckily, I had absentmindedly tucked my neatly folded piece of paper with Steve's address on it into my shirt pocket. We set off into the balmy night and I settled back into my seat to enjoy the sights and sounds as Bangkok got ready to go out and enjoy itself. It was the King's birthday in a few days time and the whole of Bangkok was decked out in fairy lights. Every tree and public building we passed was etched in lines of bulbs that lit up the night sky. About a quarter of an hour after setting off he stopped and asked to see my piece of paper again. "Okay," I said, thinking nothing of it as I handed it over. He squinted at it for a few seconds and did a lot of head scratching.

"Are we going the right way?" I asked, pointing straight ahead down the road we had been on for the last five minutes.

"Okay, Boss, Okay," he grinned at me, giving it lots of head nodding, then he promptly performed a heart-stopping U-turn across six lanes of traffic and buzzed off back the way we had come. A couple of minutes later we hauled off the main drag and zipped down a number of narrow, dark streets and alleyways before emerging on to another brightly lit main road. We drew up at the kerb and he asked me for my piece of paper again. This time he hopped out and approached a pair of men who were hunched over a game of chess at a roadside bar. Within seconds a huddle of passers-by formed around him. They included a passing pizza delivery boy, a pair of policemen, an apprentice Buddhist monk in his saffron robes, a couple of skimpy clad bar girls on their way to work and a road sweeper. This was to repeat itself half a dozen times in the next hour as we slowly groped our way across the city, and each time the action was the same. There would be much chatter and gesticulation with everyone having to read the note for themselves, and then, as if they were all being choreographed by an unseen hand, there would be an instantaneous mass pointing session. Unfortunately, nobody ever pointed in the same direction as anyone else.

Group by group and gaggle by gaggle we groped our way across the city. Two hours later we pitched up at the appointed address and the look of triumphant joy and unabashed pride on his wrinkled features was something to behold. I would wager that it was the same expression Sir Edmund Hillary gazed upon should he have shot a glance over at Sherpa Tenzing Norgay after they had just spiked the summit of Everest with the Union Jack. It said: Got you here, mate. Pure achievement.

Steve suggested that we go out to dinner, so failing to find anywhere locally we promptly hopped into a tuk-tuk and headed back into the city. Politeness dictated that I neglected to mention I had just spent the best part of the last two hours heading out of town and now here I was heading back again.

"Where are you headed after Bangkok?" he asked me, and I told him that I planned to take a ferry to the island of Koh Samui. "There are plenty of diving schools for first-timers there," he said. "Head for Chaweng, it's a bit touristy, but if you stay somewhere nearby like Big Buddha Bay, you'll be all right."

FOUR

Achtung! Achtung! – Dive! Dive!

I arrived at the port of Surat Thani at seven o'clock in the morning after an overnight bus journey from Bangkok. As dawn broke I caught my first glimpses of the lush, green tropical Thailand with Thai women riding bikes, wearing sarongs and traditional wide brimmed, conical, straw hats. At the port the ferry was waiting and I was aboard within minutes. The ferry itself looked much like the ones that years before I had used to get around the Greek islands. It had three decks and the upper one was open air and most of the handful of passengers headed for it. There was a snack bar of sorts and I bought a coffee and a sweet pastry wrapped in cellophane for my breakfast. I took them over to a long wooden bench that afforded me a view over the side. Half an hour later the ferry slipped its anchor and we chugged out into the Gulf of Thailand, the sun sparkling on the wave tops of the jade flecked turquoise sea. The port of Thong Yang lay three hours ahead of us.

There must have been about 20 or so other backpackers spread out about the top deck snoozing in the warm sunshine after the sleepless overnight bus journey. After a while they began to stir themselves and that's when the hawker went into action. He was a young Thai man and he carried a battered photo album under his arm. I first noticed him when he approached a young couple who were sitting by the stern. He sidled up to them and chatted away for a couple of minutes and then he opened the album and slowly started turning the pages. At first, I thought he was a throwback to Patpong Road and that the photos he was showing them were of skimpy dressed young women. But judging by people's reaction whatever he was offering was more innocent. Over the next hour he slowly made his way through all the passengers and it wasn't until he approached me that I realised he was selling accommodation on the island.

"You want beach hut," he asked as he sat down beside me. He started flicking through the album showing me photos of various B&Bs and rooms he had available. I had no fixed plans regarding where I was going to stay. All I knew was that I wanted a hut on a beach, hopefully surrounded by palm trees and within a coconut's throw of a bar. The one thing I did know was that even though I might not have been the most seasoned backpacker, I certainly wasn't going to be caught out by the first native property hawker that came across me, so I politely declined his offer of finding me somewhere to stay. Anyway, I had decided to follow Steve's advice and get a bus or taxi to Big Buddha Bay and see what it had to offer when I got there. I also assumed that a fair sprinkling of the other backpackers would be doing the same. My fellow passengers all looked like seasoned backpackers to me and far more experienced at this sort of thing, and if I hadn't been fool enough to be taken in by a dodgy Polaroid in a scrapbook, you could bet your bottom baht they hadn't either. He didn't seem too put out and wandered off to tick off the last couple of backpackers. So it was with no little surprise that on docking I witnessed every other backpacker being met by friendly Thai landlords before being whisked off in their jeeps to various spots all over the island, and no doubt to the pick of the best available accommodation which they had negotiated while still aboard the ferry.

Was I worried? Not a bit of it. I had a far more pressing problem on my mind. As everyone scarpered out of Thong Yang along a gravel track that led away from the landing and leaving me completely alone, I looked around to discover that the landing was in fact Thong Yang. What had been a large black dot on my map in my guidebook was in reality no more than a rickety pier and a car park in the middle of nowhere. I had a choice. I could either shoulder my backpack and set off up the gravel track and hopefully find a road at the end of it, or wait it out and see if anyone turned up when the next ferry arrived, although I had no idea how long that might be. I opted for waiting, and I didn't have to wait more than half an hour before I heard the crunch of tyres on gravel. A flat bed pickup truck drove down the track and came to a halt beside me. I coughed the dust out of my throat and looked up to see a middleaged Thai man looking at me quizzically.

"Where you go?" he asked, although somehow he managed to bark it out more like an order.

"Big Buddha Bay," I replied, not the most polite rejoinder I grant you, but something told me that his English was somewhat limited and that any further conversation was going to be conducted in bald statements rather than flowing stanzas. To take the abrupt sting out of it I fixed him with a beaming smile, which seemed to do the trick because with a grunt he nodded his head as if to say hop up. I climbed in beside him and we drove off. We drove along narrow roads that snaked through plantations, and through the fly swatted windscreen I caught glimpses of the trained monkeys harvesting coconuts from the tops of trees. They scampered up the trunks trailing long leads behind them to where men stood looking up at them as they pulled the heavy coconuts from beneath the palm fronds and dropped them with heavy thuds to the ground below.

It wasn't difficult to work out how Big Buddha Bay got its name. We rounded a turn in the road and there in the distance, on a headland jutting out into the sea, stood a giant statue of the Buddha, except that he was seated. Even from a distance I could tell it must have been at least ten metres high, and just in case you might miss it, the locals had painted the giant figure bright gold. The pickup slowed as we approached a small village which was little more than a street lined with houses, a garage and a shop. "Bo Phut," said my driver by way of introduction. The road we were driving along was no more than 30 yards from the sea, which I could glimpse through stands of palm trees. In amongst them were dotted beach huts. We slowed and turned into a narrow track. A hand painted sign was pegged to the ground bearing the somewhat incongruous name: L.A. Resort. Half a dozen beach huts with high, pitched roofs squatted in amongst the palm trees that surrounded a small beach bar and restaurant. My guy beeped his horn and the owner materialised. It was low season and there didn't seem to be many *farangs* in town. Hopefully, the owner was hungry for business and I felt the distinct possibility of being able to negotiate a very favourable rate for a change. He led me over to one of the huts that stood right by the beach. Inside it was very basic. A large bare room with two single beds and a bathroom with a toilet and a nozzle attached to a hose. He mime demonstrated that the hose served both as the flushing device for the loo as well as the shower when you held it above your head. Needless to say there was no hot water. The hut also had a large wooden veranda out front. Ten steps from the door in one direction took me through the palm trees to the beach, and another ten in the opposite direction landed me up at the bar. It was perfect, and at two hundred baht a night, ridiculously cheap. I snapped it up on the spot and didn't even bother to attempt to haggle.

There were three diving schools in Chaweng and they were all pretty similar, or so I thought. I chose Easy Divers simply because they were the nearest one to where I was staying. The diving school itself was located next to the swimming pool in the grounds of the very luxurious Imperial Boat Hotel. The centrepiece of the hotel was a flotilla of luxury apartments built to look like boats. They were undoubtedly the bees' knees inside but from the outside they looked quite ridiculous. There was a whole fleet of them frozen mid-bob on a sea of carefully manicured lawn, and when my hut cost me two hundred baht per night, these beauties weighed in at nine thousand. The Easy Divers office was unmanned except for a Thai girl who answered all my questions and told me to turn up at none the next morning for the first of my four days of tuition.

"And please read this," she said, handing me an introductory book to diving. That night I sat on my veranda doing my homework, and with the sounds of the waves crashing on to the beach only yards from my door I idly flicked through the pages. It all seemed a far cry from the Jacques Cousteau documentaries I had watched on TV as a kid. Before I'd be able to "gaze beneath ze murky waters" and "explore ze mysteries of ze deep" first of all I'd have to fathom the intricacies of neutral buoyancy and nitrogen narcosis.

Next morning I pitched up at Easy Divers on time to discover that despite its Anglo Saxon name, it was a dive school run exclusively by Germans for the large number of German tourists who visited the island. But fortunately, being early in the season, I was the only pupil and instead of being in a group of six, I would be having a one to one with my instructor for the entire week. Andreas, or Andy, as he asked me to call him, was a big man covered in reddish blond hair and looked like Boris Becker's younger brother. He also spoke faultless English. There is one thing you soon learn about all diving instructors. Previously, they have all lived very alternative lives, and usually highly stressful ones at that, like hedge fund managers or pork belly futures traders, and they've all reached a point somewhere in their lives when to escape the pressures and strains of modern living they went on their first diving holiday, and had a life changing experience the moment they donned flippers and dipped beneath the waves. Andy was no exception.

"I used to be a chef," he said.

I didn't think the Germans were particularly noted for their cuisine and was on the point of saying something glib about sauerkraut, before thinking better of it as I realised I would be putting my life into his hands over the next few days.

"What type of restaurant did you work in?" I asked him.

"By ze time I vos 25, I had three of my own," he replied. "Zey vere in Rome. Von of zem vos awarded a Michelin star. I voz... vot you call it... somezing of a celebrity."

"So vot, I mean what are you doing here?" I asked him,

"I vos verking crazy hours, I had a staff of 200 people, I vos making a fortune but vos spending it up my nose, if you know vot I mean. My girlfriend at ze time vos getting really vorried. So von day she comes to me and says, Andreas, you need to get away and relax a little or you kill yourself. She told me she had a booked a holiday for me, on my own, scuba diving. I came here to Koh Samui and fell in love with it.

"What happened to the restaurants?"

"I sold zem, but vizout me they vernt vorth very much."

"So you gave it all up to become a scuba diving instructor?"

He smiled. "Ja! Best zing I ever did. I had to pay off ze debts on ze borrowings for ze restaurants. So I vasn't left wit much money. And ze only way to continue to dive was to become an instructor."

"Probably not what the girlfriend had in mind," I told him.

"Ve broke up. But is OK, now I live with a Thai voman on ze island." He paused for a moment and then continued. "You know ze Thai vomen are very beautiful, Ja?"

On my first day I didn't even get my feet wet. We sat around a table in the Easy Divers office and Andy took me through the basics.

"Ze most important lesson to learn about diving is never hold your breath underwater," he intoned. "Ze reason for zis iz zat as you ascend, ze outside pressure gets less as you get nearer to ze surface, and ze air inside your lungs expands also." He pointed to a roughly drawn illustration in my introductory book. In a few frames it showed what he was talking about. Instead of a scuba diver it showed a balloon at various stages as it ascended. And as it broke the surface it burst explosively. "Ze zame zing vill happen to your lungs if you hold your breath underwater. So ven you are diving you must always keep your air passage open. While you're breathing through your regulator zis is never a problem but there are various safety exercises you have to perform and one of them is a controlled ascent where you share another diver's air supply. You swap ze regulator back and forth between you as you ascend remembering to let out a stream of bubbles all the time, which keeps your airway open."

As this was one of the most important things to know, Andy spent a lot of time on it and every time he referred to letting out a stream of bubbles he would say blub, blub, blub. So I spent most of my first day listening to this strapping great German guy giving me a load of baby talk.

"So, I takes out ze regulator, blub, blub, blub . . . I hand it over to you, blub, blub, blub . . .you breath in and take out ze regulator, blub, blub, blub . . . you hand ze regulator back to me, blub, blub, blub . . . I take ze regulator back and breathe in again, blub, blub, blub . . .and pass it back to you again, blub, blub, blub . . . In order to replicate getting into the habit of this we conducted the next couple of hours conversation in the same vein. "Do you want a cup of coffee, blub, blub, blub". . . "Yes, two sugars please, blub, blub, blub". . . "Where did you go to last night, blub, blub, blub"... "I tried the Beachcomber bar in Chaweng, blub, blub, blub..."

Andy had another equally unconventional but highly effective teaching method. If I got any of the basic points wrong then I had to buy him a beer, and as he said himself, "I'm German and I can drink a lot of beer," before adding a "blub, blub, blub" for good measure. The next day I squeezed into all the gear for the first time and entered the pool. My first impression was that wetsuits do wonders for the figure, and why Playtex hasn't got into the market I can't imagine. As I lumbered into the pool, replete with weight belt, oxygen tank and three feet long flippers I thought that God had got it pretty much right when pondering on where to stick us in his grand scheme of things he had ticked the dry land box.

The object of the day's exercise in the pool was to get me to take my oxygen tank off in the pool and put it on again. Then I had to do the same with my Buoyancy Control Device, or BCD. My BCD quickly became my favourite piece of equipment. It works just like a life jacket. Basically, it's a waistcoat which is linked to the cylinder of compressed air on your back and which inflates at the touch of a button. But it really comes into its own at the end of a dive when you reach the surface. Instead of treading water like mad to counter the sinking effect of your weight belt and near empty oxygen tank, you simply inflate the BCD and relax as it leaves you gently bobbing on the surface. Andy started off by demonstrating how it should be done and made it look as easy as slipping in and out of a well worn dressing gown. I finally managed it after about three hours of trying and at the end I felt like I had gone ten rounds with a professional wrestler.

"Okay," said a satisfied Andy, "tomorrow you make your first dive."

The dive boats left from a rickety pier which was only five minutes walk down the beach from my hut. Andy was there together with ten or so other instructors and about twice as many novice divers, all German. Two boats were tied up either side of the jetty. One was a sleek looking affair, all white paint and gleaming brass with a large state room and a sun deck. Ours was a converted fishing boat that was open to the elements, save for a canvas awning. The paintwork was cracked and peeling and the engine coughed thick, black, oily smoke. I rather liked it, which just goes to show how much I know about boats. It reminded me of the toy that always lies forgotten at the bottom of the toy box, the one that nobody wants to play with any more because there are lots of shiny new toys around. However, I was soon to learn that the high seas are no place for sentiment. The gear was loaded aboard, we clambered after it and we set off. It was three hours to the dive site which was a rock sticking out of the sea somewhere in the middle of the Bay of Thailand. The early morning sun was warm as we watched the island of Kho Pan Ngan, all hilly, green and tropical, slip by on our starboard side. Der Boat Meister gave us a briefing about life on board which included the request, for obvious reasons, not to use the boat's toilet while we were anchored over the dive site.

We were about two hours out when the squall struck. In the tropics these little so-and-sos pop up from out of nowhere. The sea rose, the wind whipped, the rain lashed and the swell, well, swelled. One minute I was content to chug along without a care in the world, enjoying the view and being pleasantly lolled by the motor I could feel gently throbbing beneath the soles of my feet, and the next moment I felt like I was auditioning as an extra in a low-budget disaster movie. The boat rocked and pitched violently. Forget all hands on deck, I hit it with my hands, nose, chin, chest, stomach, thighs, shins and dangly bits, and generally tried to hang on to it with any part of my anatomy that afforded even the briefest hint of purchase. I also managed to slither under one of the wooden benches that afforded the resemblance of some protection from the lashing elements. The squall passed on its way within a matter of minutes and I emerged into an eerie peace and looked around fully expecting to witness a scene of total carnage and devastation. Instead, there was the entire ship's company, instructors, divers and crew, all stood together under the awning and all looking at me with very bemused expressions. Being German I hoped that they had put my actions down to some brand of British eccentricity.

An hour later we hove to at the dive sight. A tall and fat pinnacle of rock jutted out of the sea and we anchored close by. One of the objects of diving is to see things while you're down there. Most people want to see fish, and fish tend to congregate around things like coral reefs, or in this case, large lumps of rock. Apparently, things grow on them that small fish feed off. This in turn attracts bigger fish that feed off the smaller fish. And the bigger fish attract larger fish that feed off them. And so on. All things being equal this large lump of rock sticking out of the middle of the Bay of Thailand should have ranked alongside the Coliseum in Rome for its aquatic gladiatorial behaviour.

The other thing that tends to unite divers is their love of conservation. We were sitting on deck enjoying the warmth of the recently returned sun when Der Boat Meister appeared with a laminated piece of paper showing pictures of different exotic types of fish. He sat down next to a couple and they studied it for a few moments in a huddle. The woman pointed at one of the fish, and said a few words in German to der

Boat Meister, who nodded, and then passed it on to the next person. They also studied it carefully, said a few words to Der Boat Meister, and passed it on again. And in this fashion the pretty piscatorial laminate went from hand to hand until it was eventually passed to me. The pictures showed the different types of fish that inhabited the Bay of Thailand, and which we might be lucky enough to see when we were down there. Unfortunately, I thought it looked like one of those picture menus you get for foreign tourists that I had seen outside some of the cheaper restaurants in Chaweng – and promptly ordered the one that looked like monkfish, hoping that it might come with chips. And to add insult to injury, apparently the one I had selected for lunch was one of the rarer and protected species.

Soon afterwards I was wetsuited and flippered-up and standing on the edge of the boat ready to launch myself into the wide blue under. Reaching this point had been quite an effort as getting into all my gear on a rocking boat had been a two man job. I squeezed into my wetsuit and then Andy acted as the good squire as he loaded me up with my BCD, tank of compressed air, weightbelt, regulator, mask and flippers. I felt like a medieval knight in armour waiting to be winched onto his horse. Andy had already entered the water and as I stood there teetering on the edge of the boat, he waved at me impatiently. He took his regulator out of his mouth and shouted something at me which sounded like, "Achtung, achtung – dive, dive," but I could have got that wrong. All the others had already gone overboard, and were no doubt well into their "run silent, run deep" routine in the depths below. But the prospect of sharing a three and a half hours boat ride back to Koh Samui with a full complement of Germans and having bottled it at my first attempt was enough to propel me over the edge.

I don't think my entry into the water would have earned me a five point nine from the Lithuanian judge. Momentarily, I was sailing through the air and then I hit the water, arms windmilling wildly, in a welter of froth and bubbles, the sound of my breathing through the regulator strangely loud and echoey in my ears. I didn't know which way was up but fortunately my BCD did and a few moments later I was bobbing on the surface next to a relieved Andy.

"Ve vill descend to tventy metres," he said, "and do some safety exercises."

We'd discussed this on the boat earlier and it involved filling your mask with water and then clearing it, and doing a controlled ascent sharing one diver's oxygen.

"I vant to see bubbles coming from your mouth all ze vay up to ze surface," he said.

"Blub, blub, blub," I replied. This first dive lasted little more than half an hour but it seemed to rush by. Andy released some air from his BCD and slowly slipped below the gently rippling water, and I did the same. Contrary to my expectations the hard part was actually staying below the surface. Each time I tried to descend I bobbed straight back up again. Andy quickly spotted the signs and released some more air from my BCD, which made all the difference. The key to scuba diving is achieving a state called neutral buoyancy. Underwater you are constantly trying to strike a balance between your weight belt pulling you down and your breathing, which inflates your lungs, and lifts you to the surface. So instead of going along in a straight line, beginners, like me, tend to take a more rollercoaster route. When you can go along at a constant depth, without see-sawing up and down, then you have achieved neutral buoyancy. It took a while to get the hang of it but I think I got there in the end, or at least certainly achieved a gently undulating forward motion.

As we descended the pressure built up in my ears which Andy had shown me how to clear by pinching my nose and trying to blow through it. Andy was magnified by the effect of the water through the glass of the mask, and he looked even bigger underwater than he did on the surface, which was very reassuring. I followed him down, Andy constantly shooting glances over his shoulder or twisting his body in the water with all the grace of a dolphin, to shoot a look back at me and check on my progress. The only thing I could hear in this otherwise silent, watery world was the hugely amplified sound of my breathing in my ears, and I quickly became accustomed to the rhythm of it, which helped me to breathe more slowly and evenly which in turn helped to flatten my rollercoaster progress through the water.

We slowly circled the outline of the pillar of the rock as it disappeared beneath us into impenetrable blueness, shot through with shafts of light. Dimly, I saw where Andy was leading me, a ledge about thirty metres down. As he reached it he rotated 180 degrees in the water and came to rest on it in a kneeling position, beckoning me to follow. Like a rookie pilot making his first landing on an aircraft carrier, I overshot the runway a couple of times, before Andy grabbed my weight belt and pulled me down opposite him. Then he gave me the universal thumb and forefinger in a circle sign to ask if I was OK. I remembered only just in time not to reply with a thumbs up, as this would have meant that I was in trouble and needed to get to the surface quickly. So I gave him the same sign back to tell him I was fine. Then he demonstrated how to clear his mask of water, and I copied him, tilting my head back, pressing the top of my mask to my forehead and expelling the water by breathing out through my nose and feeling it bubble out of the bottom of the mask. We had practised this a number of times in the pool, but doing it at thirty metres with the surface just a glimmer above you was another matter. Next, Andy gave me the thumbs up sign meaning that we would do the controlled ascent sharing one diver's oxygen. I gave him the thumb and forefinger sign, whereupon he promptly reached across and pulled the regulator out of my mouth. But I was ready for him, and as soon as he did I started emitting bubbles by slowly letting my breath escape. Then holding me by the collar of my BCD, he began to fin gently and slowly he began to pull me to the surface, never rising faster than the speed of our ascending bubbles. He took his regulator out of his mouth and passed it to me and it was his turn to blow bubbles. I took two deep breaths, returned the regulator back to him and blew bubbles.

And in this way we passed it back and forth, taking it in turns to breathe in and blow bubbles in a slow, underwater, vertical waltz all the way to the surface.

On our second dive we went down to look at the fishes, but the storm had churned up the water and scared them off. Judging by the subdued reactions from the other passengers on the way back to Koh Samui at the end of the day, this had been something of a disappointment. I was ecstatic though. I had just spent a couple of hours in a place that God had never designed me to be in.

Love was in the air every night in the bars of Chaweng, even if you did have to pay for it. But occasionally you could come across the real thing, or think you had. At least that was Kevin's story. He was perched on a bar stool taking occasional swigs from a bottle of Singha beer. He was the only one in the place and the bar girls at the other end of the bar were, strangely for bar girls, ignoring him. I took a stool roughly between Kevin and the girls and ordered a beer myself. In the manner of two New York barflies we got to talking and it turned out he was American anyway. Over the course of a few beers he told me his sad story. Kevin was 43 and lived in Hawaii. I can't remember what he did for a living but it involved a lot of travel to San Francisco. He had arrived in Bangkok over a week ago to meet up with his Thai girlfriend. The plan was to marry her and take her back to the States. They had met a year ago when he had been on holiday over here and this is what they had been working towards. He had got all the clearances from US immigration and was ready to go. A day after arriving in Bangkok though Kevin was struck down by some mystery bug that put him in a coma in hospital for three days. When he came out of it she was at his bedside, but her bedside manner was not all that he might have expected.

"You see, here's the real problem," he said, idly picking at the gold foil on the neck of his bottle. "She told me she had been seeing this French guy off and on over the past year but that I was the one she wanted to be with, if you know what I mean."

"So what did you do?" I asked.

"Well, I asked her about this French guy and she told me that he had been over here a few times and that she had even been to stay with him in Paris."

"So was it now over with him?" I asked.

"Not exactly, you see while she was seeing him she got pregnant and she's gonna keep the baby."

I let that sink in for a moment or two and then said, "Does the Frenchman know that she's pregnant with his child?"

"No, at least that's what she told me, you see she still wants everything to be as it was with her and me before this happened," he said.

"But surely she knew she'd have to tell him some time," I said.

"Yeah, well, I guess that was why she was having it all out with me beforehand to see what I was gonna do."

"Keeping her options open, you mean," I said a little nervously not knowing how he was going to react to me taking a somewhat cynical view of his girlfriend's attitude.

"Exactly how I figure it," he said to my relief. "You see a lot of these Thai girls when they get hooked up with a foreign guy they wonder if the guy's ever gonna show up again. It makes 'em pretty insecure I guess. So when another one comes along it's a pretty good insurance policy to have."

"Maybe, but it hardly smacks of true love, if you don't mind me saying so," I said.

"You're right," he said. There was a long uncomfortable pause as he called over the barman and ordered us another couple of cold ones. "You see, I just don't know any more if she really wants to be with me, or if I'm just a ticket to a better life in the States and someone to bring up her kid."

"This great show of honesty at your bedside might have been calculated just to win you over and make you feel sorry for her," I said. After all, she wouldn't be able to hide the pregnancy for long, so she really had no other option but to tell you." There ensued another long silence. "So, what are you doing here on Koh Samui?" I asked him.

"Well, as soon as I got out of the hospital, I felt I just wanted to get away for a while and think about it all, y'know."

"I don't blame you," I said, anybody would. "But what happens to her if you don't decide to marry her and take her back to the States?"

"I don't know," he said.

"Can she raise the child on her own in Bangkok, does she have a job or a family that will support her?" I asked.

"That's not it," he said. "She told me that the Frenchman is flying in next week to see her, that is if I don't take her back with me."

"Does he know she's pregnant with his child?"

"No, or at least that's what she says."

"And you believe her, because again she could just be keeping all her options open," I said, and in a way I could understand her motives.

"You know," he said with a sigh, "I don't know what to believe any more." I realised it was not just his own future he was considering. Whatever he decided to do would fundamentally affect the lives of three other people.

"Any idea what you're going to do?" I asked him.

"I already know it's not gonna work," he said. "I could forgive her the French guy I think but it's the kid I can't handle. I just don't want to raise another one."

We had a couple more beers and talked about this and that. He said it had been good to talk it through with someone and I suspected that it was better that it had been a stranger who he would never see again. As I walked back to my beach hut that night I thought about a desperate

Thai woman whose life had promised so much but was now in total disarray, a Frenchman who was about to arrive in Bangkok and get the biggest shock of his life. And just because she had kept him as her second option was no guarantee that he would look after her. Finally, there was Kevin, a nice enough guy who in a few days would be flying home to Honolulu where a gathering of family and friends would be waiting at the airport to welcome him and his new bride, except chances were she wasn't going to show. I felt sorry for them all. I saw Kevin again a couple of nights later. He was in another bar further up the street but this time he was the focus of attention of three young Thai women. I walked by knowing that having poured his heart out to me he probably didn't want to see me again, and in such company. I let him be.

FIVE

A Hop, Skip and a Jump

If you have ever played ducks and drakes on a day out at the seaside, skimming flat-sided stones across the surface of the sea, you'll get the idea of my trip through Singapore, Hong Kong, Brisbane and Sydney. They were short staging posts on my way to the USA. Having enjoyed the back to basics existence of a beach hut for the last couple of weeks, I was looking forward to a change of scene and swapping waking up to the sounds of surf washing up on the beach to the "quissssssshhhhh" of a cappuccino maker. After all, there's only so much Robinson Crusoe a north Londoner can take. The person who was going to reintroduce me to the world of the mod con for a few days was Julia.

Julia and I had worked at the same advertising agency back in London, and being far more talented, clever and hardworking than me, she had landed herself a plum job a few years ago at one of Singapore's top ad agencies. When we had worked together Julia had been an account director. Account directors have very difficult jobs as they have to be the link between the client, who is the one who pays for the advertising, and the creatives, who are the ones who do the advertising. Unfortunately, the two seldom see eye to eye.

In my day clients generally tended to view creatives as talentless, ego-tistical prima donnas who wouldn't know a piece of popular thinking that ordinary people could actually understand if it jumped up and bit them in the nether regions. While creatives looked down on clients as unimaginative, corporate Neanderthals whose sole *raison d'etre* was to unquestioningly approve vast shed loads of cash in order to bring their artistic visions into being, especially when it involved a three week shoot in Tuvalu for a varicose veins commercial. Anyway, the point being that Julia was extraordinarily gifted at reconciling these two opposing forces which she did with a grace, tact, charm and a ruthlessness that any serving foreign secretary would happily trade his or her eye teeth for. Her particular skill was to win a client's complete trust, and many were the meetings when an exasperated client would simply turn to her and say, "Julia, what do you think?" And whatever Julia said, simply went.

Not being the most colourful crayon in the creative pencil case, I was at least smart enough to make sure I worked on as many pieces of business run by Julia as possible. The woman was brilliant at her job and anyone who worked with her couldn't fail to look good. I grappled her to my soul with hoops of steel. Julia's other defining characteristics were that she was great fun, hugely popular and generous to a fault. So generous in fact that when I first planned this trip and emailed her, her immediate reaction was to invite me to come and stay.

Coming into land at Changi airport, Singapore's role in the world was clearly defined in a glance out the window. Singapore exists on trade, and I had never seen so many tankers and cargo vessels gathered in one place. Big jobs too and the sea was dotted with them for miles. Many of them must have spent as much time finding a parking place offshore as they did getting there from far-flung places like Valparaiso in the first place. Beyond them rose the skyscraper offices of the international banks, multi-national companies and hotels that made up the Central Business District, or CBD. Flying into Singapore was like arriving at a twenty-first century Venice, but without the prospect of a being able to get a decent ice cream.

Like a lot of people I always feel guilty walking through customs when I haven't even bought any duty free, let alone have anything to declare. My Lonely Planet had told me that Singapore was a strict little society to say the least. On the Khao San Road I'd heard horror stories of straggly-haired hippies arriving at Changi only to be frogmarched by immigration officials straight to the barbers to get a short back and sides, but these may have been apocryphal. So when the customs official fixed me with a steely look it sent shivers up my spine. Brace yourself old son, I thought, here comes the old strip search. He is going to march me off to a small room, snap on a pair of industrial strength rubber gloves and start probing parts of my anatomy that will go pop when he takes his finger out. But fortunately he waved me through. I swept across the gleaming marble floors of the airport, stood in line next to a group of impeccably well dressed Singaporeans, waited my turn to hail one of the spotless taxis waiting in the rank, and when my turn came headed off to Julia's apartment, which was located near the southern tip of the island. We drove along freshly swept roads which were bordered by rows of small flowering plants neatly arranged like so many hundreds of thousands of little soldiers on parade. The palm trees were of a uniform height and all the fronds looked like they had been trained to droop at precisely the same angle. This was obviously a highly ordered society. Even the flora didn't dare take a step out of place.

Julia was out at work but her amah, Filipino housekeeper, knew to expect me. The apartment was large and open plan, and the highly polished, dark wood floor was cool under the soles of my bare feet. I padded across it to check out the view passing heavy, mahogany furniture which fought with Indonesian native sculptures and potted tropical plants for floor space. The terrace was wide and overlooked a communal swimming pool. The apartment managed to be stylish, ethnic and colonial, and all at the same time. That night we sat up late drinking wine and catching up, even though Julia looked tired.

"So, what's the advertising business like in Singapore then?" I asked.

"Much the same," she replied. "Today it was one long battle between the Singapore government who want a recruitment campaign for the navy and the creative department who are hellbent on turning any TV commercial into a glorified video game."

"What does the client say to that," I said.

"Oh, they just asked me what did I think."

No change there then. Every morning Julia disappeared off to the office at a frighteningly early hour, and a few hours later I stirred myself and commuted to the pool, where I spent the best part of each day. I only stirred myself from my sun lounger to re-enter the apartment and enjoy the delicious lunch Julia's amah had prepared for me. On the one occasion I did stir myself and go and have a look at Singapore I found it to be a very pretty kind of bland, a very clean type of bland, and a very polite, safe and well-ordered type of bland. But at the end of the day bland is always, well, just bland. I'm probably doing Singapore a great injustice, and I know many people who think the place is the business. It's incredibly clean, it's safe, and a number of single women travellers have told me it's their favourite place in South East Asia because they feel they can go out at night on their own. Perhaps I had just been too knocked out by the teeming, crowded, grubby excitement of India and Bangkok to appreciate Singapore for what it had to offer. All the time I was in Singapore I felt like I'd been shrunk and I was walking around an architect's model of what a modern city should be, and that if I looked up I'd see huge pairs of eyes staring down at me.

About two weeks before I arrived in Singapore, Raffles had just completed a multi-million dollars refurbishment programme. Nice of them to go to all that trouble, I thought, but I was only popping in for a drink. Consequently, the place was even more spotless than the rest of Singapore, if that was possible. One could only guess at how badly it was in need of a refurbishment before, perhaps a waiter had accidentally spilled some coffee on the carpet on the stairs. Of course, the place to go in Raffles is the Long Bar, the home of the Singapore Sling. As it was lunchtime I slugged back a couple of Tiger beers instead. The room was elegant, old-style colonial with lots of potted palms, wicker back chairs and paddlewheel fans that turned slowly on the ceiling. As the barman topped another Tiger for me I was almost beginning to feel relaxed for the first time in a public place in Singapore, and then I noticed something extraordinary. I rubbed my eyes and looked again, and yes, it was still there. Could it be true, was the floor of the bar covered in litter? On closer inspection I saw that they were peanut shells, dozens of them. Apparently, it was one of the traditions of the Long Bar that you cracked open peanuts while sipping your cocktail, and as a special dispensation you were allowed to casually drop them on the floor. This was too good to be true, so even though I am not a great fan of peanuts, I indulged myself by breaking open a few just for the sheer pleasure of throwing the shells around. I resisted the temptation to start flicking them off the chandelier just to get that satisfying little "ting", as I thought that might be pushing my luck. Anyway, the place may have had a relaxed attitude but there were limits as to how far they were prepared to go. You may have been allowed to drop your peanut shells on the floor at Raffles, but every couple of minutes or so a little woman would dart out of nowhere with a dustpan and brush and scoop them all up.

Hong Kong

Chek Lap Kok sounds like an East European table dancing club. Actually, it's one of the world's most sophisticated, hi-tech, international airports, and as such it is very much a symbol of Hong Kong. It was all space-age light and vast open areas. It was super-efficient and felt as if every passenger's passage through the airport had been choreographed and split-timed by some unseen army of time and motions people hunched over a battery of spreadsheets and behavioural analytics pie charts. When I walked into baggage reclaim and up to the carousel I swear my backpack drifted up to me on the conveyor just as I arrived. I also had the bizarre feeling that if at the last minute I had detoured and gone to the toilet on the way, it would still have arrived at the same time as I did. Customs and immigration were a breeze, too. Hong Kong is a business city, and in the world of business time is money, so nothing gets in the way or holds up the international dealmaker on his, or her, way through.

From the airport it was a twenty minutes journey on a sleek silver train into the heart of Hong Kong. Even this didn't throw Chek Lap Kok's precision timing out of whack. As soon as I stepped onto the train the doors slid closed behind me, and the moment my bum hit the seat we slid away from the platform and out of the terminal.

Twenty minutes later the shuttle came to a stop at Central, the doors slid open and I stepped out and on to the platform right in front of where Anna was standing. This efficiency thing was beginning to get a bit tiresome. But it was great to see her. Years ago Anna had joined the agency as a young recruit and had worked her way up through the ranks of the media buying world, negotiating airtime deals with some of the toughest negotiators to be found in any business. Then she had left to join a large international media buying outfit and was now in Hong Kong for another media buying giant as their Director of Planning. Anna was Italian but had been raised in the UK. Professionally she had the world at her feet, and having inherited the striking good looks that Italian women are famous for, probably had half the male population of Hong Kong grovelling down there as well. She bundled me into a taxi and half an hour later we pitched up at her apartment building. Anna lived in a side street by one of Hong Kong's landmarks, the Happy Valley racecourse. We entered the building through a ground floor car park and stepped into a small lift. I say small, I've stood on street corners and made telephone calls from inside boxes that were larger. Space was at a premium in Hong Kong and every square inch mattered. A floor tile's worth of space saved in the public areas like the lifts and landings meant an extra floor tile's worth of space you could charge for in the apartment. Not that this made the apartments in Hong Kong particularly spacious. As I stepped into Anna's living room I checked the walls for the tell tale claw marks, where a cat had tried to get a grip while they were testing the theory of whether or not it could be swung in it.

But by Hong Kong standards Anna's apartment was big. I got a more graphic example of this a couple of days later when I asked Anna what were all the little boxes that jutted out from underneath many of the windows. She explained that many of the apartments in Hong Kong also had live-in Filipino *amahs*. They normally slept in the kitchen, usually on a mattress on the floor, and that these little boxes that jutted out from the walls were the extra space for their feet. Anna's apartment didn't run to an amah, what it did have though was a six-feet-six beanpole of a fellow media buyer called Constantine, who was Dutch and who shared the flat with her. They often attended media functions together, and with Anna being a perfectly formed five-feet-four they must have made a noticeable couple. Once when he left his door open I got a peek inside his room. It was tiny. I wondered if instead of an amah's window box, he had a similar arrangement where perhaps the end of his bed disappeared through the open doors of his wardrobe and his feet slept under his Armani suits.

I arrived on a Saturday night and Anna was in the mood to go out and party. We strolled down to the end of her street and hailed a cab that took us to Lan Kwai Fong, the upbeat downtown of Hong Kong. It was buzzy and trendy and full of even more glamorous expats and young Hong Kong Chinese, and all of them seemed to have the latest model mobile phone permanently stuck to their ears. Elegant young men and women wearing designer names sipped designer drinks in designer bars, all the while peering over the rims of their designer sunglasses to check out who was wearing the latest designs. Hong Kong had any number of nightspots where the ex-pats larged it. We hit Carnegies. The place was heaving when we arrived. It was a small, compact bar where a resident DJ played seventies and eighties classics, and it was jumping. One of the traditions here was to boogie on the bar. In the past they had a couple of unfortunate accidents where revellers completely lost it and fell from a not inconsiderable height onto the bar staff. But rather than ban the practice, the management instead had the good sense to install a crash barrier, like you see for holding back the crowds along the mall on the Queen's birthday, along the entire length of the bar. Partygoers could still clamber up and do their stuff while the bar staff could continue to serve drinks through their legs, secure in the knowledge that they were not going to be crushed by a flying merchant banker.

Next morning we took a taxi over the peak to Stanley on the other side of the island. On the way we passed one of the strangest buildings I have ever seen. It was a large, square building perhaps 12 stories high and looked like any 1960s style provincial office block back home, except that there was a large hole in the middle of it, about three stories high and four rooms across. It was a void, there was nothing there, just a huge square hole surrounded by building like a concrete, steel and glass doughnut.

"What on earth is that," I said.

"Extraordinary, isn't it," said Anna. "Apparently after they built it the feng shui man came round and told them that it was blocking the path of the dragon who needs to come down to the water's edge to drink. So they had to knock a hole in it."

I wondered if it hadn't been one of the firms of architects who lost out on the bid to build the thing in the first place. What was to stop them, I mused, paying off a dodgy feng shui master to give it the evil eye so to speak. Then next time they pitched for a job they only had to point out what had happened last time they weren't appointed, and I reckon there wouldn't have been too many clients who would fail to recognise the unspoken threat – "Give us the contract or we send our feng shui scam man round."

At Stanley we wandered down to the water's edge and watched one lonely guy on a surfboard trying to get upright before the frostbite and the wind chill factor did for him. And further out to sea a sole waterskier ploughed a lonely furrow across the waves. We did the sensible thing and repaired for lunch at a Thai restaurant and wolfed down plates of steaming noodles. In a vain effort to walk them off we strolled around the craft and souvenir market, all pretty touristy. Stanley reminded me of a British seaside town, out of season, only the food was better.

Anna decided it was easier to catch the bus home, especially as I had said that I wouldn't mind being dropped off in the centre of Hong Kong, and going for a walk around. We took seats on the crowded top deck and Anna realised that as I would be making my own way back to her apartment from the centre of Hong Kong, I would need a quick Chinese lesson so that I could tell a taxi driver where to take me. The thought hadn't occurred to me. No wonder they had made her Head of Planning.

"The area where I live is called Pam-a-day," she said.

I repeated it a good few times until it was rolling off the tongue with all the familiarity of ordering my regular, post-pub Friday night take-away.

When she was happy I was up to snuff on that one, she said, "And the name of the street is Yuk Sow Guy".

This one didn't come so crisply off the bat at first. The Yuk bit was pronounced as in "look" and I was saying it as in "luck", the Sow was as in the female pig and I was sow-ing as in throwing seeds around, but on the Guy bit I was getting straight As. It took me quite a few stabs to string both of them together correctly, but finally Anna gave me the nod. It was then that I looked around and noticed quite a few pairs of inscrutable Chinese eyes staring at us. "Jeez," they seemed to say, "are those guys on the wrong bus, or what."

Hong Kong is one of the most densely packed cities in the world. Nearly everyone lives cheek by jowl in apartment blocks, and most of them have resident *amahs* living and working in them. Sundays are the *amahs* only day off, and not surprisingly they like to get out for a bit, and they do, in their tens of thousands. The streets were simply lined with thousands and thousands and thousands of petite Filipino women. Their ages ranged from 16 to 60 and all they did was chat; all of them, and all at the same time. Sundays are an institution for amahs, it's the one day of the week when they can catch up with family and friends, talk about home, discuss the latest gossip, swap news and letters, complain about their bosses, laugh, joke and cry. Every street I turned into the pavements were covered with hordes of them sitting on steps, in door-ways and on the pavements. They perched themselves on low walls, clung to railings and swarmed over steps. There was not a bare patch of ground to be seen. And the noise. They may have split up into groups of anything from four to a dozen but whatever the size of the gathering they all spoke at the same time. It was like a scene out of Alfred Hitchcock's *The Birds*, but made with sparrow like little women. I didn't begrudge them though. They worked very hard all week, sent every spare cent home to support their families, and spent their one day off indulging in the cheapest possible form of entertainment known to man, or rather woman, having a good old gossip.

I spent five days in Hong Kong and on every one of them I crossed the harbour on the Star Ferry. It wasn't a ride, it was a pilgrimage. In the new towering steel and plate glass city of Hong Kong, which Has been Chinese for many years and what the government calls a "special economic zone", the Star Ferry is one of the few remaining links to the Hong Kong of old; a slightly sleazy world of clogged streets and opium dens, where merchant adventurers and inscrutable Chinese lived cheek by jowl with rickshaw boys and bar girls. The merchant adventurers were still there, of course, only now they call themselves merchant bankers live in the luxurious, high-rise apartments of mid level. Trading in exotic spices and silks has been replaced with betting on spot prices in the commodity and financial markets. Deals were no longer hammered out, face to face, in the confines of a captain's cabin of a junk bobbing at anchor in the harbour, and in the spluttering light of an oil lamp, but were done on touch-screen computers with faces lit by the rainbow glow of mul-ti-coloured screens. The technology and commodities might have been different, but a nineteenth century merchant adventurer would have had no trouble recognizing what was going on today – trade, and at any cost.

Wheeling and dealing has always been in Hong Kong's DNA since the first junk sailed into the harbour, even if it is junk bonds which sink without trace. Whether one of the thousands of traders, arriving in the business district in his or her silver BMW and already negotiating the first deal of the day on the latest touch screen smart phone, were too busy to notice the oddly-shaped, twin-decked vessels that had just pulled away from the jetty, I couldn't say. The Star Ferry has been making the crossing from Hong Kong island to Tsim Sat Shui in Kowloon on the Chinese mainland for just over a hundred years, so perhaps it was understandable that Hong Kongers might take it for granted.

I bought my ticket and walked down a ramp and waited with dozens of other passengers in front of a high gate that looked like a drawbridge in front of a castle, except that it didn't swing out but went vertically up and down. A loud bell sounded and it rose to admit us onto the ferry. The ferry had a lower and upper deck, which called to mind that other world-famous icon of public transport, the London Routemaster double-decker bus. It seemed to be just as popular with ordinary passengers as well and not just the handful of tourists who also clambered aboard with me. The lower deck was enclosed so I elected to ride upstairs. Hard wooden benches crossed the deck and there were wide standing areas which served just as well for the tourists wanting to enjoy the view as the hordes of commuters who still used the ferry during the rush hour. As we left the ferry terminal in Central on Hong Kong Island I half closed my eyes and looked back at the waterfront of the Wanchai area. The babble of Chinese echoed all around me and I let my imagination roam to try and recapture a fleeting glimpse of the world of Suzie Wong. In the novel, the bar girl of the title first meets the English artist, Robert Lomax, on the Star Ferry. By chance he ends up staying in the hotel where she "works", unaware at first that it's really a thinly disguised brothel for wealthy expats. He promises himself not to dally with any of the bar girls who work there, preferring to befriend them and become a part of their "behind the bamboo curtain" existence, the better to paint and record their life. But Suzie takes a fancy to him, and despite the fact that he practically acts as her pimp in setting her up with another English man resident in the city, the inevitable happens and they fall in love, which the reader knows will happen from the moment Lomax first glimpses her on the Star Ferry. They escape Wanchai, get married and live happily ever after. Highly improbable as storylines go, it depicted Suzie as the archetypal "tart with a heart" and was made into a film in 1960 with Nancy Kwan taking the title role and William Holden as Lomax. And given its sweetly sentimental portrayal of what must have been in reality a pretty sordid life, I've always wondered what Frank Capra would have made of it.

The next day I went off in search of the world of Suzie Wong, having been told that the fictional Nam Kok Hotel, where most of the action takes place, was based on the Luk Kwok Hotel in Gloucester Road in Wanchai. The novel was written in 1957 and little remains of Wanchai as it was then. I walked down Gloucester Road where concrete and steel highrise office blocks had replaced the more traditional buildings of the Suzie Wong era. Wanchai's sleazy romanticism had been bulldozed and replaced by towering edifices of government sponsored respectability. I walked past the Immigration Tower and the Revenue Tower which rose sheer into the sky, and the Hong Kong Convention Centre was an all-together very different embodiment to doing "business" in Hong Kong. Standing in front of the hotel itself, which had been redeveloped in the 1980s and renamed the Gloucester Luk Kwok, I looked up and my heart sank. It was yet another very modern, very smart, very state-of- the-art business hotel that rose floor after floor high into the overcast sky. The novel describes the original building as being something of a ramshackle colonial affair built in the 1930s, and I had always imagined it to have looked like Raffles, but gone to seed. Inside the reception area was hushed and imposing and exuded an air of business efficiency, and the marble walls echoed to the *click-clacks* of business people as they crossed the highly polished floor. The sordid had been replaced with the soul-less, and knowing which I preferred I turned on my heel and left quickly before my cherished memory of the world of Suzy Wong was blotted out by the world of the international business traveller, never to return. There was only one thing to do, take my farewell trip across the harbour on the Star Ferry.

Brisbane

"Here for the cricket are ya', mate?" asked the taxi driver who picked me up from Brisbane airport.

"No, not at all," I replied. For my sins I happened to be in Australia while England were touring on a five-match-test series.

"Well the boys are sure to rip the piss out of you anyway, especially after they've had a few beers," and with that he roared with laughter and turned his attention back to the road. Welcome to Australia, Pom.

In the back seat next to me Tricia shot me a sympathetic glance, which I thought was the very least she could do. After all, if it hadn't have been for getting drunk with Tricia back in the Harringay Arms in Crouch End I wouldn't have embarked on this round the world odyssey in the first place.

Tricia had booked me a room in a hotel in downtown Brisbane right on the river which she called "the units" when she told the cab driver where to take us. This conjured up in my mind an Aussie version of those Japanese commuter "rooms" I once saw in a documentary, where people get to lay their heads in cubicles little bigger than telephone boxes laid on their sides and stacked up on top of one another like a rack of pigeon holes. But when we got there I was pleasantly surprised to find it was like a small apartment in a block that stood on a sweep of the Brisbane River. I stood on my balcony and the view to the right looked down on the highrise offices of the City Business District, but was dominated by the Story Bridge, an ugly looking iron girder affair which I didn't mind at all as it looked like the kid brother of the Howrah Bridge in Calcutta. While to my left the south bank was given over to recreation with landscaped parks, a wooded tropical walkway and a vast landscaped public swimming pool. Further along stood an arts development that boasted an art gallery, concert hall and a museum, and Tricia told me that the whole kit and caboodle was a legacy to the city from an Expo held years before. The river was broad and blue, and powerful-looking ferries called Citycats prowled up and down, criss-crossing the river to pick up and discharge school kids, shoppers and office workers.

Tricia was staying with her brother Paul and his wife Mary and their three kids, so with a cheery, "Enjoy yourself, darl," she left promising to pick me up tomorrow to take me out for a what the locals apparently called a "Sunday arvo".

That night I popped into a local pub called Kelly's. It had a tin roof, no carpet and bare walls, except for the odd beer poster and calendar showing pictures of girls who had forgotten to put their shirts on. There were three pool tables at the back, and in the corner a four-piece band played old Jethro Tull numbers from the seventies and Irish reels. It wasn't crowded with drinkers and there were no women. Most of the men wore beer-stained, sweaty vests and shorts and they huddled round the bar territorially. This saved them a lot of walking back and forth as their beer glasses never seemed to be empty for long. Let's just say it didn't strike me as the sort of place where I would feel comfortable elbowing my way up to the bar, and in a loud voice proclaiming, "I say Landlord, fetch me a foaming tankard of your finest ale, and be quick about it my good man." Not until we had won at least one test match anyway.

Brett Wharf, where Tricia took me for lunch the next day, lived up to all my expectations of the Australian dining. The restaurant was set on the bank of the river way out of town and we dined outside under the shade of a large canopy. The speciality of the house was a towering platter of fish, not unlike a fruits de mer. I lost count of the number of different varieties of shell food, and other seafood, that was placed before us, but I do remember especially enjoying the curiously named Moreton Bay Bugs, which when they arrived weren't unlike grilled sardines, only with a meatier, fishy flavour. The broad terrace was packed with diners dressed in t-shirts, shorts and thongs, but despite that the cuisine and service was of a standard I would have associated with one of the posher London restaurants.

What followed though proved to be a total contrast yet was no less Australian for all that. On the way back into Brisbane we stopped off at the Brecky Creek Hotel. The "Brecky Creek" was a big Victorian looking lump of a place, based on a two-storey Queenslander house. It was built of yellow bricks, with brown pillars, and it had a wide veranda running all the way round it which featured lots of fancy white painted iron trellis-work. It also had a gently sloping corrugated iron roof that looked like a slouch hat that had been pulled down low to afford maximum protection from the relentless sun. I was a little taken aback by this stop over because the Tricia I knew back in the UK wasn't a great fan of pubs, and as she explained this was down to places like the Brecky Creek. It seemed she was making something of an exception in my honour. I knew that before she'd left Australia to come to the UK she had been an actress, what I didn't know was how she had tried to take culture to the outback.

"We'd go on tour for weeks on end," she told me. "After each performance the cast would repair to the local pub, but the problem was I was the only girl, and was never allowed in, so I'd have to sit outside on the steps, like I was on the naughty step."

So it was with no little sense of sacrifice that she led me inside. It was a rollicking great beer hall of a place that was packed with Aussie swillers hell bent on boozing their ways through their Sunday afternoon, the "arvo". At one end was the bar, where two barmaids were kept on their toes slinging beers down the counter like they were working on a factory production line.

"Things have obviously moved on a bit since your days," I said to Tricia as I pointed out some ladies sitting at some tables and chairs that lined one of the walls. Otherwise the place was almost devoid of any furniture.

Instead, wrought iron leaning rails had been bolted to the floor at regular intervals, like the crash barriers you used to get in the days of football stands before all-seater stadiums became law. They gave the men things to lean on and dozens of guys were propped up on them as they chugged back glasses of frothy looking lager, and meant that more drinkers could be crammed into the bar.

The language was a bit ripe and could only just be heard above the din of the pokies, or fruit machines. The noise level was of bedlam proportions, and as if all this wasn't enough, televisions bolted high up on the walls poured forth a stream of excited horseracing commentaries. This meant the men had to shout at the top of their voices to order rounds of beer, which were matched for level by the raucous put-downs by the girls behind the bar who were serving fifteen to the dozen and giving as good as they got in the verbal stakes at the same time. Any attempts at conversation were going to be a non-starter, so having managed to order a couple of beers, Tricia headed for the pokies faster than a cold one disappearing down a stockman's throat at the end of a cattle drive. It just went to show, you can take the girl out of Brisbane but you can't take…

As well as giving us the Sydney Opera House, Australia's other great contribution to the architectural heritage of the world has to be the *Queenslander*. It's a house, and a very special type of house at that. Queenslanders come in all shapes and sizes, and are very individual, but they all share certain characteristics that make the Queenslander a type. They include wonderful wrought iron work on balconies and balustrades and they all possess broad verandas. However, the most remarkable thing about Queenslander houses is their portability. How could I tell? Because we had just turned a corner and we almost ran into one, which was jacked up on the back of a huge lorry, and was being driven down the road at a sedate pace.

"We could be here a while guys," said Tricia who was sitting in the front seat next to Dianne who was driving. Dianne was one of Tricia's oldest friends who was also a Brisbanite but had moved to New York many years ago and was back visiting. A lawyer by trade, Dianne had a somewhat more unconventional view of life and lived and worked as an artist amongst other things. She was represented by a gallery on the Gold Coast who sold her strong, vibrant canvases to visiting Japanese tourists for serious amounts of money. Wherever she was in the world, Dianne would get an email saying that the gallery was running out of stock and could she get her brushes out. Dianne would then lock herself away for a few weeks, knock out half a dozen large canvasses, roll them up and stuff them in a large cardboard tube, and DHL them to the Gold Coast where the gallery would frame them, hang expensive price tags on them and hang them on the wall. When they sold, Dianne was sent a fat cheque. We were on our way to visit Dianne's mother, Heather, who lived outside of the city near a place called Beenleigh.

"What are the stilts for?" I asked.

"They're called stumps," said Tricia, "they let air circulate under the house in the dry to help keep it cool, and in the wet they provide protection against flooding."

I suspected they had another purpose. By being a metre off the ground perhaps they afforded some sort of token resistance to all the various forms of biting insects and reptiles that no doubt took up residence underneath them. If architecture speaks to us, then I think what a Queenslander is saying is, Look, here's the deal, you get to crawl and slither all over this nice shady patch we've created for you, and we promise not to go down there and disturb you guys. But, in return, I don't want to see any of you emerging from the overflow in the bath, especially when the lady of the house is in there having a soak. And that goes double for any visiting poms, OK. The other thing about the unique design of Queenslander houses is that it must make them great fun to buy. Being portable and built on stilts they can be lifted up, transported and dropped on any patch of relatively flat land. We had passed a number of house lots along the way. They were just like used car lots except that they were a lot bigger, and featured rows of houses for sale instead of motor cars. The way it worked was you bought the land separately, and then went in search of a house to plonk on it. You then simply plugged it into the local electricity and plumbing supply lines. As a concept I thought it had a lot going for it. Don't like the view from the bedroom window, twist the house round to face the trees. Noisy neighbours, shift the house to the far end of the garden. Of course, all this was a lot easier said than done, and it took an industrial crane, a wide-berth trailer and a lorry that could tow a jumbo jet to do it, but it looked like it could be done. I thought it also brought a whole new meaning to the term "moving house".

Heather's house, which was also a grand looking Queenslander, when we eventually got there, wasn't in the bush exactly but sort of bordered it. The house stood in a few acres of land dotted with stands of eucalyptus trees. As we drove up the rough track that led to the house a small group of wallabies bounded along the track next to us like an official escort. It was early evening, and the sun had lost its fierce glare and was just pleasantly warm. Even so I didn't feel entirely at ease. This was my first foray outside of the relatively civilised comforts of Brisbane, and before I embarked on this trip I had watched a natural history programme on TV back home, entitled *The Ten Deadliest Snakes in the World*, and from memory it seemed to me it had been shot almost entirely on location in Australia. If Australians can be counted amongst the most welcoming people in the world, then their wildlife certainly can't. Australia has more things that can kill you, that either slither, crawl, swim or spin webs, than any country on earth. So it was with no little trepidation that I stepped gingerly out of the car and bounded over the six feet or so of scrubland that separated the car from the sanctuary of the house.

"G'day, Bob," said Heather after she had hugged her daughter and was being introduced to me by Tricia. Heather was tall and slim with silver hair and cut a strikingly elegant figure. I immediately complimented her on her beautiful home, which, it has to be said, was spectacular, but I really had to get the snake thing off my chest before I felt I could relax.

"Tell me, Heather," I asked, "do you get snakes at the bottom of your garden?"

"Strewth no, Bob," she replied.

"That's all right then," I said, breathing a sigh of relief

"Oh no, they come into the house now."

She was quite serious. Apparently, the poor little things got horribly hot during the day and liked to cool off on the tiles of Heather's hallway. She told me she was quite used to coming home from work in the late afternoons and shooing them away, probably in much the same way as I habitually got rid of the next door neighbour's cat from my doorstep. The difference was that each one of Heather's little interlopers contained enough lethal toxins to take out a small herd of buffalo. It was a good job she worked in a hospital.

Heather had managed to make my intrepid journey into the heart of the almost outback very agreeable by laying on a spectacular feast, which was washed down with copious amounts of fine Australian wines that we had stopped and bought on the way at the appropriately named grog shop, which is what they call off-licences in Australia. So much so that if I had have been bitten by something long and slithery I probably wouldn't have felt it anyway. But each time I left the veranda where we were dining to go to the bathroom I took a golf club with me from the stack that Heather kept inside the front door, just in case. This amused everyone hugely. The chances of me encountering something angry, coiled up on the marble tiles and having a hissing fit we probably quite remote. So too were the chances of me being able to land it a good fifty yards away in the equivalent of the middle of the fairway with a trusty seven iron. But it made me feel safer though.

But, of course, Australia does have its friendlier fauna, or so I thought, and you can't be lulled into a false sense of security than by being told that you're going to cuddle a koala.

"You'll love it," said Tricia, not bothering to conceal a cackle of laughter as she added, "I'm going to take a photo to show everyone when you get back."

The Lone Pine Sanctuary was an hours ride on the Citycat out of Brisbane. The sweeping curves of the river slid by and it wasn't long before we left the city in our wake and almost in an instant the office blocks gave way to rich people's houses which nestled in their privately owned, lush, green patches of tropical jungle. The guys who drive the Citycats must have the most frustrating jobs in the world. They drive big, powerful, sleek machines that ply their trade up and down the broad Brisbane river all day long and at a speed that never exceeds what I could only call a pootle. The temptation to push those throttles forward and let that sucker go must be at times have been almost overwhelming. I dreaded to think what carnage would ensue if one of Bangkok's long tail boat ferrymen was ever let loose behind the wheel.

To distract himself from such thoughts our Citycat driver kept up an impromptu commentary on the history of Brisbane as seen from the river. At one point our driver pointed out a house that was the scene of a gruesome murder, and it did look remarkably like the Bates Hotel from the movie *Psycho*. As we approached a particularly large sandbank the boat slowed right down. Unlike their immediate neighbours the trees were largely bare except for large black pods that hung from the upper branches like hundreds upon hundreds of big burnt salamis. They turned out to be fruit bats, big ugly brutes that gave me the shivers.

"That's the Regatta Hotel," he said over the PA as we slipped past a Victorian period looking property which boasted a wide veranda overlooking the river. "It's famous throughout Australia," he intoned, "because it was here that a group of Sheilas chained themselves to the railings as part of a protest campaign. But they weren't after the vote. Nah, they were after the right to drink in a public place."

"Yeah," added Tricia, "and don't think that this took place in the 1860s, it was actually in the 1960s." On more than one occasion she had referred to Queensland as being the Deep North. I was beginning to understand why.

The Lone Pine Koala Sanctuary didn't look like anything like a zoo, it was landscaped and spacious, and boarded walkways wandered through it. Australia being a very hot country, its animals don't seem to do very much if they can possibly help it, especially in the early afternoon when we visited. At least this meant they couldn't be bothered to run away when you approached, so I got a good close up view of some of Australia's most exotic specimens which included platypus, lorikeet and kookaburra, which sadly couldn't be bothered to sing in the old gum tree in which it perched. My favourite animal, more for its name than anything else, was the hairy nosed wombat, which looked like a cross between a rabbit and a particularly scruffy wire-haired terrier. And yes it had a hairy nose. Meanwhile, back at the branch, a large lizard was doing absolutely nothing at all so we wandered off to feed the kangaroos. They were obviously more than familiar with the drill. A dozen of them were penned in a special enclosure and we were invited to buy bags of feed for them at twenty cents each. The bags contained half a pound of little green pellets. The kangaroos lay on their sides on the grass, propped up on one elbow waiting for the tourists to approach and feed them. They looked like so many rotund senators at a Roman banquet. Mind you, I'm not so sure I'd have been that tempted to bound around in the forty degrees heat for only a handful of green pellets either. The only time they stirred themselves was when the emus tried to muscle in on the act, and only then did they actually do a bit of bounding, amazingly, seemingly in slow motion.

There was no mistaking the stars of the show though. "This is Anja," said the smiling keeper, a young woman in her early twenties, "and like all koalas she's very shy so you have to handle her carefully. In fact, koalas don't really like to be handled but she's quite used to it, and they only do it for a few hours a day and get plenty of days off."

Then she took me through the handling drill.

"You have to stand very still or else you might spook her," she said, "in fact I want you to imagine you're a tree."

Not having been to RADA, I made the best stab at the tree acting thing I could muster. "Now I want you to place both hands together in front of you over your belly to form a cradle, and keep your hands under the koala to support her the whole time." I did as I was told and she gingerly placed Anja on my chest. Koalas are incredibly cute. They're infectiously cuddly and Anja looked at me with eyes that swim with trust and gentleness. She slowly lifted an arm and hooked it round my neck to a chorus of "oohs" and "aahs" from the others waiting in line for their cuddle.

"The last instruction is the most important of all," said the keeper, "take a big smile." And with that she produced a camera and took the obligatory photograph. I was allowed a five minutes cuddle with Anja and the girl gave me a few facts about Koala life as I held the warm ball of fur. "Koalas live off eucalyptus leaves which are 50% water, and the word koala comes from the aboriginal language, and means does not drink," she told me. This made koalas a pretty ironic symbol of Australia I thought. But there was no mistaking the particular joy of holding a koala bear and no one seemed immune to their charms. In the restaurant come canteen the walls were lined with photographs of the great and the good who had been to the sanctuary and cuddled a koala. They included Jacky Chan, Eric Clapton and the Queen Mother, looking like a little girl with her first pony. They all mugged outrageously for the camera, and even Mikhail Gorbachev had been snapped gurning like a good 'un as if to say "the Russians are cuddling".

The next morning Tricia came in the taxi with me to the airport for my flight to Sydney, from where I would take an overnight flight to Los Angeles. Tricia would be flying back to the UK a few days later and we arranged to meet in the Harringay Arms as soon as I was back to complete the full circle of my round the world trip by having a drink in the very place it started. I paid for the coffees and the waiter, noticing my accent, said "Bad luck, mate, did you see our boys pissed all over you in the final test." But by then I was well past caring about the cricket. Thankfully, in America they've never heard of the bloody game.

SIX

Go East Young Man

Most Brits travelling to America fly west and land at New York or Boston or Orlando or somewhere else on the eastern seaboard. I felt I was sneaking in through the back door. I didn't have any accommodation booked, but in America they have a pretty good system. In the concourse at Los Angeles Airport, or LAX, stood a bank of courtesy phones, and above them illuminated boards that featured ads for all the local hotel chains. I phoned around a few to compare rates and finally settled on the Days Inn on West Sunset Boulevard. It was in the part of LA where I wanted to be, close to the Walk of Fame and within relatively easy reach of Hollywood, Beverly Hills and Universal Studios. It was also only $59 a night, which by LA standards was pretty cheap. I picked up the phone, dialled the toll-free number and was told that they had a room and that if I waited outside the terminal a Days Inn courtesy bus would be along to collect me in ten minutes. I waited underneath a flyover and ten minutes later the Days Inn courtesy bus duly arrived. Half a dozen of us assorted travellers climbed aboard.

"Where y'all goin'," shouted the driver over his shoulder as he gunned the engine and lurched into the steady stream of traffic. In turn we called out the addresses of the various Days Inn motels we had chosen, and he mentally plotted a route dropping us off in order. Even though I was one of the first to be dropped off it took nearly an hour to get to Sunset Boulevard driving along wide, fast highways. The first glimpse I got of LA wasn't encouraging. It was flat and seemed to have no civic heart or downtown area, a sea of suburbs looking for a town centre, and all laced together by wide six lane motorways. It also looked vast and seemed to go on and on for miles and miles in all directions to disappear into featureless horizons. Bedford Falls it certainly wasn't.

My Days Inn was a cheap motel-ish sort of place but it had a pool and my room was small and basic which suited me fine. That afternoon I went for a walk to get my bearings and check out my immediate surroundings. Sunset Boulevard itself held none of the magic which Gloria Swanson's film of the same name had given it. First of all it wasn't a boulevard at all. It was just a rather long straight road that went on for miles and was lined with fast food outlets. One block up I found the Walk of Fame. Most of the names etched into the purple stars inlaid into the sidewalk were familiar to me from movies and TV shows, and I was surprised to see that it also included music and rock stars, where we Brits seemed to figure quite strongly. In order to get your name down, literally, you have to be invited by the Los Angeles Chamber of Commerce who are the people who decide whether or not you are worthy of the honour. Then, if you are selected, you get the privilege of handing over a few thousand dollars to have your name engraved and the distinctive star inset into the pavement. I strolled over Jack Nicholson, Marlon Brando, Tom Cruise, Elton John, Elizabeth Taylor and many more, including Demi Moore. Some of the greatest egos on the planet were there, so it was satisfying knowing that they had all paid a small fortune for the privilege of letting me walk all over them.

"I beg your pardon, Sir." The man behind the counter at the Days Inn reception struggled to keep the incredulity out of his voice but he failed miserably.

"How long will it take me to walk to the Sunset strip area," I repeated. He scratched his head and stared blankly back at me. I might as well have asked him to explain Faraday's third law of motion for all the sense I was getting out of him. It was the word walk that had thrown him. Nobody walks in America if they can possibly help it, especially in LA.

"I can get a cab here for you in under a minute," he said reaching for the phone.

"No thank-you," I replied, "I prefer to walk."

He swallowed nervously. Everyone in LA was steeped in film culture, just like I imagine everyone in Grimsby knows all about trawler fishing, so no doubt having been brought up on *Psycho* he was probably thinking that in the Hitchcock thriller, wasn't it the motel owner who was supposed to be the deranged loony, not the guest.

"Walk?" He still wasn't getting it.

"That's right," I said. "Is it far?" He never actually answered the question. Instead he pointed vaguely up the street. The strip was really just more of the same, except there were a few more slightly exclusive looking bars and fast food restaurants dotted in amongst the malls and burger bars. So it came as something of a surprise to see a British pub. I sat on a bar stool inside the Coach and Horses and listened to the barmaid tell one of her regulars that she had only recently had the braces removed from her teeth and that she would soon be swapping this job for the film offer she was sure her bright, shiny, new smile was about to win her. At the other end of the bar a guy was hitting on a party of four girls who were dressed for a night out, even going so far as to give each one of them his business card as they beat a hasty retreat, saying that he worked for a studio. Perhaps it was true because when I left half an hour later he was outside talking to the bouncer and I overhead him say, "I still have one good friend at Fox," before slipping him a card, too. It seemed everyone in LA was trying to muscle in on the movie business.

I hadn't found anywhere to eat but remembered there was a Mexican place called El Cantina opposite the Days Inn, and so decided to look in there on my way back. It was karaoke night in the El Cantina, and as I tucked into a plate of fajitas and tacos I must have heard

You're The One That I Want – in Spanish – at least three times in the space of half an hour. The place was done out in an adobe wall effect, with a brightly tiled, blood red floor and heavy wooden hacienda-style tables and chairs. I ordered a beer and stood at the bar and tried to ignore the singing. I glanced across at a girl who was sitting on her own at a table near the bar and who looked as if she was in her late twenties. Her hair was dark and was tucked through the loop at the back of a baseball cap to where it hung down between her shoulders in a ponytail. She wore dark glasses, a leather biker's jacket, silver rings on every finger, baggy blue jeans that were cut-off mid calf, and white ankle socks on tiny feet that were tucked into sandals that were far too large for her. She looked up just at that moment and without a moment's hesitation said, "Hi, what song do you want?"

"Oh, I don't come to karaoke bars to sing," I said, totally misunderstanding her. "Not unless the management want the place cleared, that is."

"You're funny," she said bursting into a staccato peel of high pitched laughter. "No, you pick one and I'll sing it for you." Whether or not she twigged my accent I don't know, but by way of encouragement she added, "I know a lot of songs by the Beatles."

I opened the songbook lying on the table in front of her and picked out *Ticket To Ride*, which seemed appropriate for a traveller.

"How about that one," she said totally ignoring my suggestion and jabbing her finger at *Can't Buy Me Love*.

"OK," I said, "*Can't Buy Me Love* it is, but I warn you I know all the words so I'll know if you make a mistake." This solicited another machine gun ratatat of laughter. "You're soooooooooo funny," she said again. "Can I have one of those," she added, pointing at my bottle of Bud. Adding, "I'm Lisa-Maria."

She got up, crossed over to the microphone that stood on a small stage and as the familiar strains of the Lennon and McCartney classic swelled she promptly began to murder it. I managed to keep her talking for most of the next hour, so she only got up a couple of times, once to massacre

Hey Jude and on the other occasion to annihilate *Yesterday*. I'm sure everyone else was grateful for my efforts because I'm pretty sure I detected an almost imperceptible en masse groan each time she headed for the microphone. On the other hand it could have been the sound of John Lennon turning in his grave. When the bar closed up Lisa-Maria promptly invited herself back to my hotel room to watch TV.

"Ah, that could be a bit of a problem," I said, "there's a notice in reception saying that guests have to leave the rooms by eleven o'clock."

"You're so funny," she said bursting out laughing again. "This is California, we don't do rules here. Except maybe in Orange County," she added as an afterthought, which was completely lost on me.

Bold as brass she led me across the road, straight through reception and into room 205 with me trailing haplessly in her wake. Apart from the double bed my room had a chair and a wardrobe and that was about it. And as there was really nowhere else to sit but on the bed she slipped off her jacket, t-shirt and jeans to reveal a pink bra and matching knickers and promptly sat cross-legged on the bed in that easy comfortable attitude that all California girls have. She picked up the TV remote and started flicking through the channels. In Sydney I had got rid off my last remaining Australian dollars by buying assorted bags of sweets and chocolates. She made a beeline for them and sat half naked on my bed, transfixed by a variety of game shows, shovelling down things called Cherryripes like they were going out of fashion. As there was nowhere else to sit I lay down beside her. By the time we were reaching the climax of *The Price Is Right*, and the couple from Indiana were um-ing and ah-ing over whether or not to take the money or go for the agricultural rotavator, I couldn't stand it anymore and made my move. But when I say move I somewhat flatter the manoeuvre. It was more of a lunge really. She squealed and dissolved into a fit of giggles and pushed me off saying, "You're funny." I gave up and slipped under the covers while she continued to flick from game show to reruns of *I Love Lucie*. I must have nodded off because the room was dark and quiet when she slipped in beside me. The next morning, as we walked through reception to go to breakfast at a diner across the street, we didn't escape the receptionist. "People aren't allowed in guests rooms after eleven o'clock," she said tapping the sign the way school-mistresses used to tap blackboards with a ruler. Without missing a beat Lisa-Maria checked her watch and without a backward glance said, "What's the problem, it's only a quarter after ten."

We crossed the street to one of the fast food places where we had a breakfast of pancakes and biscuits covered in gravy. Lisa-Maria got talking to the guy in the next booth, then casually said good-bye to me and went and joined him.

On the Beverley Hills tour we were told we only had half an hour to explore Rodeo Drive, which was probably just as well given that I couldn't have afforded a cup of coffee there. It was definitely a case of window-shopping only, but at least you got to gaze upon lavishly expensive things, which was more than what we got to do on the tour of the stars' homes. This was the highpoint of the tour where we were bussed around the glitzy suburbs of Beverly Hills and Bel Air, where the who's who of the Hollywood rich and famous lived. Trouble was you didn't get to see anything at all of their homes. What you did get to see though was their very expensive security. At each house the only clue to the residents' wealth and standing in the Hollywood community was given by the height of their security gates and the number of CCTV cameras they had bristling at every corner. Quite a few had armed guards, too. I wouldn't have been surprised if they had tank traps inside as well. So I didn't learn a great deal about Mel Gibson's taste in domestic architecture, but I can tell you that his wrought iron gates are bigger than Nicholas Cage's. Despite the fact that Hollywood stars guard their privacy with a vengeance, they probably welcome the tour buses. Should any canny thief ever manage to slip past the guards, scale the electrically wired walls under the all seeing eyes of the security cameras, circumvent the alarm system and manage to lift the impressionist masterpiece off the wall without tripping the maze of invisible laser beams and make it outside with the booty, it will all be to no avail because the getaway driver will never be able to make it through the throng of tourist buses clogging up the immaculately swept boulevards.

At the last count LA had something like twenty-six million cars, which is more than most countries have people. Car parks under some of the buildings in LA go down ten floors. Five thousand Rolls Royces are registered in Beverly Hills alone, and twenty-five percent of all of Porsche's international sales come from California. Some years ago the city authorities tried to do something about the resulting smog problem and decided they had to encourage people to stop using their cars. Fat chance. Anyway, undeterred they built an eight mile long stretch of underground railway at a cost of three hundred million dollars per mile. But nobody uses it for fear of earthquakes.

At this point I have to admit it wasn't solely *It's A Wonderful Life* that had inspired me from boyhood to visit the USA. I grew up to be one of those old school film buffs who venerate that most American of cultural icons, the western. For many of my generation it defined America in the eyes of the world. Repeats were always being shown on TV and I grew up watching classic westerns like *The Searchers*, *Red River* and *Rio Bravo*, not because they all starred John Wayne but because they were great movies. Even the non-classics had great moments. *Destry Rides Again*, which happened to star James Stewart, has got to have one of the best fight scenes ever committed to celluloid. Two hundred cowboys knocking seven shades of cow dung out of each other in a saloon bar brawl of epic proportions, and all in one great big master shot; chairs crashing through windows, bottles being smashed over heads and the piano player bashing away at the honky-tonk in the corner and never missing a note as cow-pokes went cartwheeling over his head and out through the double swing doors. And not a CGI effect in sight – now that was the art of film-making when Hollywood was great. But the lasting image is of the tough, noble, self-reliant hero who became just as much a part of the American cultural landscape as the mesas and buttes that punctuated the plains and canyons he rode through on his ceaseless knight errand's quest. And no-where more so than in the movie *Shane*, which established a genre of storytelling that has yet to ride off into its final sunset. If you took Luke Skywalker, dressed him in fancy duds and a white hat, swapped his light sabre for a sharp shooter, put him astride a stallion rather than in the cockpit of a star fighter, and threw him up against a horde of Mexican *bandidos* rather than a bunch of the Empire's storm troopers, you'd have a classic western.

Growing up in Kenton, Middlesex, Star Wars wasn't around in my day, but *The Lone Ranger* was on television when I got home from school. Played by Clayton Moore, the first actor I ever hero worshipped, every week he would ride into some wild west town with his trusted Indian scout, Tonto (we weren't politically correct in those days, so there was no mention of words like Native American) and right whatever wrongs that needed righting. This always involved The Lone Ranger fighting for truth and justice in the good old American way. He was quick on the draw and his six-shooter fired silver bullets. And every episode began with a deep, booming voice over uttering the immortal words, "A fiery horse with the speed of light, a cloud of dust, and a hearty 'Hi-Yo, Silver! The Lone Ranger rides again!" Well, now it was my time to leave the city behind and head out into the wilderness. But instead of "A fiery horse with the speed of light", I opted for a red family compact from a car rental company with a speed of not very much. Basically, I opted for the cheapest class of hire car available, with the proviso that I could return it at any other dealership nationwide as I hadn't decided on my route yet.

All I knew was that I had three weeks to go lose myself in the great American landscape.

The lure of Highway 1, otherwise known as the Pacific Coast Highway, which runs from L.A. to San Francisco and hugs the coastline the whole way making it one of the truly great drives in the world, proved irresistible. But first I had to get out of one of America's vast cityscapes, and this meant negotiating L.A.'s cross-town traffic. The problem was I had to get across a busy three-lane road to turn left at a set of traffic lights in order to join the freeway. And from the junction where I joined I only had a quarter of a mile in which to cross over the three lanes of downtown traffic, which was a river of fast moving bumper to bumper metal. On my first attempt I didn't even manage to get out of the inside lane before my turn-off went hurtling past and I had to take a slip road, double back in a circle and get on it again. The second time I managed to get into the second lane before I missed my exit and had to double back. It was the same story on the third, fourth and fifth attempts and I was beginning to feel dizzy. There was nothing else for it, I decided, the only thing to do was ignore whatever was coming up behind me, floor the pedal to the metal and go for it. So on my next attempt I hit the gas, rammed the indicator arm down and left it there; determined to cut my way across the three lanes of fast moving metal in a single swathe. I was doing fine until I lost out to one of those big rigs hauling a trailer that could have come straight out of *Smokey and the Bandit*, and I did a double take just to make sure Burt Reynolds wasn't behind the wheel. On either side of the cab, twin exhaust funnels belched angry clouds of smoke, and its wheels were as high as the roof of my car. I can verify this because I got an extreme close up view of them as it became obvious that we were heading on a collision course and that if I continued my cross-lane trajectory we would very soon be sharing the same space. Not a good idea. I let discretion be the better part of valour, missed my turning, and shot off down the slip road again while the truck driver saluted me with a teeth-rattling blast of his horn and the finger.

Eventually, I made it onto Highway 1 and headed out of the city via Venice Beach and Santa Monica. On my right hills rose in shades of tawny brown and were cut by the canyons where the rich people lived in multi-million dollar properties. I drove into one of these canyons just for a looksie. It went nowhere and looped back to the coast road again. It was just like a suburban crescent and the only purpose it served was to link a number of secluded ranch and hacienda-style houses. All of them were walled off, gated and bristled with CCTV cameras. They had paid a fortune to enjoy a view of the Pacific, and I wondered if they ever managed to catch a glimpse of it over their security. I wondered if this may have been the ghastly legacy of Charles Manson. I seemed to remember that he went on his killing spree in a place like this. I rejoined the coast road and drove for another hour with the Pacific Ocean sparkling on my left. I stopped for lunch at a roadside diner in Malibu and then went for a walk along the beach as big winged birds of prey circled overhead. The beachside properties were all built on stilts and as I walked I watched sand pipers and dippers patrol the water's edge on thin spindly legs and play kiss chase with the waves that washed up around them, chasing them back into the sea as they receded then scampering back up the beach again every time a new roller crashed in. Behind me nobody rich and famous living in the beachside properties tapped on the window and invited me in for a cup of tea.

Someone had told me that when Delta flights fly into Santa Barbara the flight attendants make this announcement, "If this is your first visit welcome to Santa Barbara, and if you're lucky enough to live here, welcome home." So I had understandably high expectations as I drove in along the coast road in the early evening, just as the huge orange orb of the sun was setting over the Pacific. My Lonely Planet told me that cheap accommodation was to be found at the International State Hotel on State Street, which was easy to find. I parked the car kerbside by a pay phone and punched the relevant numbers. The room was small and only just had room enough for a bed, a table and chair and a washstand. I shared a bathroom down the hall. But the price was a good deal and they even threw in free juice, coffee and doughnuts for breakfast.

What I hadn't taken into account were the railroad tracks that ran by the hotel which I drove over when I arrived. You'd have thought that a nice little town like Santa Barbara would have been more than adequately served by a branch line. *Au contraire*, the railroad track turned out to be the kind of arterial railway line where trains half a mile long and bearing names like the West Coast Super Chief and the Continental Flyer plied their trade. The significance of this became apparent at about 3.00 in the morning. I had opted for an early night so as to get my first impressions of Santa Barbara in the clear light of day. So I was sound asleep when the room started to vibrate. I flicked the light on. Already the very faint line of dust that coated the furniture had started to lift. As the rumble built to a roar so the light bulbs began to rattle in their sockets. The bed started to judder like it had just been plugged into the mains, and then it began to shuffle off across the room towards the window. And all of this was before the approaching train's whistle blew. Shrill? Actually, the train's whistle was strangely reassuring. This being California, my first thought on waking had been that it was the San Andreas fault having a seismic tremble, having patiently waited over a hundred years for me to check in.

Next morning I went for a stroll and it didn't take me long to realise what Delta flight attendants mean. Emerging from the hotel I turned right towards the ocean. The morning was crystal clear and the pale gold of the early morning sunshine was already warm as I walked the five minutes down State Street that took me to Stearns Wharf. When I walked to the end of it and looked back I understood what all the fuss was about. First there was the deep blue of the Pacific Ocean. Its waves lapped onto a broad beach of fine white sand, which even at that early hour was peopled by sun-kissed, golden-haired Californians "takin' some rays" and playing beach volleyball. A line of tall puffball palm trees separated the beach from a broad boulevard, where open-top Porsches and Mustangs purred up and down. Then came Santa Barbara itself. The town is built completely in Spanish Colonial style and all the buildings are painted white or pastel salmon shades, and topped with terracotta tiles. Behind the town, the gated houses of the rich and famous, which rival anything I had seen in Beverly Hills, rose in steps into dark green hills. And behind these thickly wooded hills stood the Santa Ynez Mountains, a low-lying range that protects the town like a giant arm swept around it. Even the weather is near-perfect all year round. And every year migrating whales choose a patch of ocean just off shore to spawn. There's no other word for it, the place is blessed.

From Stearns Wharf I strolled up to the marina, where millionaires' yachts at anchor bobbed in the wakes of fishing boats that were putting out to sea. On the way back to my hotel I passed a postman who must have had the best job in the US Mail Service if all he got to do was walk around Santa Barbara all day. I decided to take a leaf out of his book and abandon the car. I headed up State Street which ran all the way from the foot of Stearns Wharf into the downtown area. It was home to a cluster of bars, restaurants and chintzy shops. Just off State Street I happened across Santa Barbara's oldest building. The Casa de la Guerra dates from 1820 and is a sprawling adobe ranch style house built on three sides around a dusty courtyard. For a hundred years or so it was where the *Patron* held court, and I imagined it was exactly the sort of place Zorro would have lived in while playing the fop. Just round the corner was its modern-day counterpart, the County Courthouse, a striking yet bizarre looking building that eschewed all symmetry, and which would not have looked out of place in Gaudi's Barcelona. It was here that I met Trolley Tom. Perhaps his job was slightly better than the mail man's in that they both got to go around Santa Barbara all day, but at least Tom got to drive. He was a thick set fellow in his mid fifties and he drove the local tour bus which had been decked out to resemble a street car trolley, the kind that Judy Garland rode in the musical *Meet Me In St Louis* while singing "Clang, clang went the trolley – ding, ding, ding went the bell". I joined a group of Japanese tourists and hopped aboard.

"The Mediterranean Spanish look," Tom told us, "was only started in the 1920s. Before that Santa Barbara looked more like Toledo, Ohio, than Toledo, Spain," he said with a chuckle.

"What strikes me about Santa Barbara," I told him, "is that for an American city its remarkably lowrise."

"That's got nothing to do with conservation, Bob, it's to make sure the houses on the hills behind the town get a clear view of the ocean."

"A case of money talks?" I asked.

"Sure. And talking of money did you know that Santa Barbara is one of the richest areas in America with one of its highest per capita incomes."

As we drove around the perfect streets, passed perfect houses in the perfect sunshine I discovered there was a laid back classiness about Santa Barbara. The people who lived the American dream here weren't on the make, they had clearly made it already. Trolley Tom then told me by the mid eighties Santa Barbara had become so desirable that in order to protect its exclusivity the city authorities had passed a law restricting its population growth and pegging it at 850,000. To keep the place nice for the residents the city authority went so far as to install automatic sprinkler systems in the municipal grass verges, so that they stayed nice and green all year long. But not everyone in Santa Barbara was living the American dream. Behind the scenes, digging the drains, cleaning the hotel rooms, changing the linen, parking the cars and manning the laundries was a small army of Hispanics, and I got the impression that should there ever be a shortage of laundry maids and gardeners then the city authorities would quickly turn a blind eye towards a small rise in the Mexican American population.

Driving up State Street we passed a bar called Q's. "That's the biggest bar on State Street," Trolley Tom told me, "and it used to be a mission for alcoholics. "So don't let anyone tell you we Americans don't possess a sense of irony."

But drinking had become a lot more civilised in Santa Barbara, sophisticated even, as I learnt when I headed up into the Santa Ynez mountains to visit the wine country.

"Chardonnay, Syrah and Merlot do particularly well here," explained Bion Rice, the proprietor of the Sunstone Winery.

Bion was tall, blond, tanned and I guessed in his late twenties. He wore a t-shirt, faded jeans and sneakers and looked like he should have had a surfboard tucked under his arm. Instead he was gently swilling a pale golden Viognier around the bowl of a large glass. He was typical of the new breed of new-world wine maker: young, immensely knowledgeable and passionate about wine. Sunstone was just one of the many independent wineries dotted throughout the Santa Ynez Mountains.

"We call them mom and pops," Bion explained, "small family run wineries. My mom and pop started this when they got the idea after a trip to Provence. It's all about the local geography," he went on, "because what we have here is a micro-climate. Santa Barbara stands on the only one hundred mile stretch of land along the whole Pacific Coast that runs east-west. It's perfect for growing grapes."

I took another sip and agreed with him. Bion talked a good game and he had the patter, well, off pat. We were standing in the cool of the cellar which had been cut like an extended cave into the side of a hillside. Huge barrels of tawny coloured French oak lay in rows almost touching the dome of the ceiling. As we swirled, sipped and tasted he used words like "buttery structure" and "fruit and citrus nuances". But he clearly knew his stuff and proved to be a very amiable host as he escorted me round the property. The main building was a Spanish style hacienda faced with the pale golden stone that gave the vineyard its name, and the vines grew on gently rolling hills that were bathed in soft Californian sunshine nearly all year long. Many of them didn't call themselves vineyards at all, but wine ranches, which I preferred because it gave them a distinctly western air.

"We're completely organic here, and every Sunstone wine is a product of a vineyard which respects the importance of the earth's cycles," Bion told me as his guided tour came to an end. At the Sunstone Winery near Santa Barbara the wine wasn't just chilled, it was cool.

So too were the bars on State Street and after dark they buzzed. Sharkeez was a lively young surfer's bar and restaurant that was designed in a Salvador Dali meets Nike sort of way. Across the street, the Santa Barbara Brewing Company was a micro-brewery that served beers brewed on the premises, and reminded me of the bar the sit com *Cheers* was set in. While Joe's, further up State Street had a more neon chic that was straight out of the movie *American Graffiti*. I had never thought of the Americans as having much of a drinking culture but how could you not like a town that had the word bar in its name not once, but twice. What really impressed me was how efficient the bar staff were, and when it comes to pulling pints we can learn a lot from the Yanks.

The bar staff were always on the move. When they weren't serving customers they were washing and stacking glasses, or polishing the bar counter, or smashing up ice, or practicing those spins and twirls with the cocktail shaker that impress the ladies so much. I noticed this sitting on a bar stool nursing a Santa Barbara Blond, which was a beer, not a babe. I bet you can sidle into any bar in America and almost as soon as you've settled on to your stool the barman will be in front of you saying, "What can I getcha!!!" They're not being rude, it's that their energy levels are running so high. In a lot of British pubs the place can resemble the Marie Celeste on a wet and windy Bank Holiday and you still have to cough up a lung to attract the attention of the barmaid. Walk into any American bar and order a beer and chances are you'll be greeted with a machine gun burst of: "We got Miller, Coors, Budweiser, Amstel, Heineken and Bud Lite." And that's only the draught ones. And with the speed and dexterity more normally associated with matadors delivering the *coup de grace* in the *Corrida*, the barman will have thrust a menu in front of you while simultaneously running through the list of that day's specials. American bar staff know their stuff too, and bar work in America is, quite rightly, a skilled job requiring the proper training. You can't just walk in off the street and start serving drinks as I did when I was a student. Not only can your average American barman rattle off the constituent parts of every cocktail from A to Z, they can produce them in front of your very eyes in a dazzling blur of upturned bottles and flying ice cubes. Cruising the bars of Santa Barbara I reckoned the Americans have got it about right, they're slick whereas all too often we're just slack. On my last evening I sat on the terrace of the Endless Summer bar, overlooking the yachts in the marina as the sun set in shades of orange. All around me the beautiful people were strolling, chatting, texting and flirting. I had picked up a local newspaper earlier in the day and opened it at the classified ad pages. This is always a good ruse if you want to get a fix on a place. The classified ads will tell you more about a community than anything else. They'll tell you what work people do, how much they get paid, what they drive, what style they live in, what they shop for and what they get up to at weekends. Santa Barbara was no exception. But it went one better. Nestling amongst the job and real estates ads was one that offered a $10,000 reward for the safe return of Lucy, a missing Yorkshire terrier. I wondered if this tasty little morsel of information about Santa Barbara life might one day end up in Trolley Tom's commentary. I also wondered whether or not Lucy's owners realised that they might have just unwittingly invented the dog-napping business.

After *The Lone Ranger*, a whole series of western TV shows galloped into my young life: *Wagon Train*, *Gunsmoke*, *Laramie*, *Rawhide* (starring a young Clint Eastwood as Rowdy Yates), and *The Virginian*. And like lots of other kids in the playground I thought the TV western had reached its apotheosis with *Bonanza*, and then *The High Chaparral* came along.

The series was set in the Arizona territory during the 1870s where the fictional Cannon family, led by Big John Cannon, battled to build a cattle ranch in the desert scrub. It had all the hallmarks of a classic western but beneath its dusty, heat soaked escapism there lurked a sense of realism too. The scripts actually addressed themes like racial conflict, and in some episodes the local Apache were actually the good guys. This was unheard of stuff, and the skill of the writers meant that these issues fitted into the storylines as smoothly as a .38 into the chamber of a Smith and Wesson. But what drove the show were the characters – Big John, Buck, Blue Boy, Manolito and his fiery sister and Big John's wife, Victoria. They were a world away from the stereotypes I had grown up watching. They were flawed and they fought just as much amongst themselves as with roaming bands of vaqueros that terrorised the range, but never enough to break the underlying bonds of loyalty, love and friendship that bound them all together.

My High Chaparral was called the Alisal Ranch. Actually that's not strictly true, its full name was the Alisal Guest Resort and Ranch, and it boasted a swimming pool, two eighteen hole golf courses and a restaurant where you were expected to wear a tie for dinner. I had the distinct feeling that it would turn out to be a lot more Palm Springs than the *Ponderosa*, but then who did I think I was kidding. I had never been on a horse in my life and if I was going to do the cowboy bit without breaking a limb, I figured it had better be on a ranch of the five-star dude variety.

The Alisal was a couple of hours drive from Santa Barbara and my map told me that a short detour would take me to the Cold Springs Tavern, an original stagecoach stop on the Wells Fargo route. I slunk off the main road and followed a two-lane blacktop which snaked through wooded hills for a few miles. There was no mistaking the Tavern, a couple of low slung log cabins nestling in the trees by the side of the road, and it looked like I wasn't the only one passing through. Thirty or more gleaming

Harley Davidsons were parked up outside like a line of dominoes. I squeezed my little red Ford compact at the end between a strip pole fence and the first of the shiny chromed monsters, and just caught my door in time as I opened it to stop it knocking over the first bike and watching horrified as it took out a few hundred dollars worth of assorted, high-end, show room quality motor bike machinery.

A crowd of Hell's Angels was milling about the veranda and the patch of ground in front of it. Most of them were big men, middle-aged and with grey beards that curled over their paunches. They ambled about wearing cowboy hats, dark glasses, scruffy Levis and sleeveless leather jackets, some with confederate flags stitched onto them. There didn't seem to be any headless chickens running amok. Instead some of them carried paper plates piled with dollops of hummus and falafel burgers with piles of bean salad. One of them with a guitar perched on the steps and started strumming, but instead of delivering a blood curdling rendition of *Bat Out Of Hell* he mournfully sang along to a Leonard Cohen song, which he followed with a medley of Dandy Livingstone hits. It seemed the only devil in evidence here was the one Suzanne had to be beware of. Being the only one not dressed in an ensemble of denim and leather I immediately stood out but they went to great pains to make sure I was made to feel welcome and I was greeted with a mixture of smiles and nods.

"Hi, how are you today, I'm Randy," said a particularly small rotund specimen of the breed, extending a pale, podgy hand. "This is my wife Sandy," he added indicating a very pleasant looking woman who stood next to him wearing a Guns 'n' Roses t-shirt.

Randy and Sandy? They had to be kidding me. We got talking and Randy told me that he worked in real estate and that his wife was a nurse. He introduced me to a few of the other hombres that made up his chapter.

"Ron there works for the city," said Randy nodding at a pair of 50 year olds in aviator shades, cut off denims and red and black bandanas that were knotted over what I suspected were thinning pates. They raised their bottles of Bud back at us in acknowledgement. "And Henry works in dental supplies." They wandered over and joined our group and it soon became apparent they were more interested in what I did for a living than the life I happened to be living that took me to the Cold Springs Tavern. It was like attending a meeting of a local Round Table that had somehow morphed into a ZZ Top convention.

"You know that movie," said Sandy to their bemused faces after I had explained the mission behind my quest.

"Yeah right, the one they always show at Christmas on HBO, said Henry with a smile that could have doubled for an ad for the products he sold.

"So what about you boys," I asked, "ever feel like cutting loose, ditching the day job, hitting the road and living the dream?"

They looked at me as if I was a couple of cylinders short of a V8. But then again to be fair to them I didn't exactly look like what I was representing either. When Jack Kerouac wrote *On The Road* he hitched his way into the heart of the American dream, working on farms and at gas stations and the like as the need took him. A poncey voiced English-man with a Ford compact and a credit card didn't really cut it in their eyes, and I couldn't blame them. But at least I was doing it full-time and not just at weekends. As I took my leave, I passed another biker who wore a tee-shirt with a message printed on the back that said: If you can read this then the bitch has fallen off. But the rest of the week I bet he jumped to it every time his wife told him to take out the trash.

I got in the car and reversed out – very gingerly – and headed for the town next to the ranch for a look around. Solvang sounded more like it. The name had that frontier town twang to it like Durango. Admittedly, I didn't expect a one horse town with a general store, a corral and a saloon complete with hitching post, but neither did I expect to drive past quaint looking gingerbread houses. The buildings were all of dark wood, with steeply pitched roofs and pretty painted window frames with shutters that had hearts and spade motifs carved into them, and the balconies overflowed with gaily painted window boxes. Solvang, it turned out, was modelled on a Danish village and looked decidedly more Hansel and Gretel than Butch and Sundance.

If the Alisal was anything to go by, then California's version of the Wild West experience was a lot more laid back than some of the working dude ranches I had heard about, where you paid a small fortune for the privilege of spending ten hours a day "movin' those beeves" with as much ropin', and brandin' thrown in as you could handle. I quickly got the drop on the place and figured that the clientele was largely made up of city slickers from LA and San Francisco who were more than likely wanting to chill out rather than saddle up. I checked in late afternoon and met up with my "companeros" in the restaurant, where the pre-dinner drinks were gin and tonics, not shots of red eye, and when the conversation, when it got round to the subject of shooting straight, was more a case of, "I shot a round of eight four and birdied the ninth". But maybe all that would change tomorrow at first light. I had booked myself to go on the breakfast cook out ride.

Rising at "sun up", actually I was buzzed awake by the bedside alarm, I was one of the first down at the corral, and there, big as life, stood a proper cowboy. Sam Switch was the Head Wrangler at the Alisal, and he was tall and rangy and he spoke with a slow, easy drawl.

"Heh Barrrrrb, how're doin?" he said after I introduced myself. Sam was dressed in blue jeans, a plaid shirt, a curly-brimmed straw cowboy hat and tan boots. He looked the real deal except for a small goatee beard and round rimless glasses favoured by a certain breed of interior designer. Like a couple of cow pokes we got to talking while we waited for the others and I asked him how he came to be at the Alisal.

"I was born in Pennsylvania," Sam told me, "but I left there when I was 17 and headed for Wyoming because I'd always wanted to work with horses. I didn't have a job to go to, so when I got there I just bummed around ranches doing whatever I could to persuade people to give me some work, any kind of work, didn't matter so long as I was on a ranch. Then someone gave me some good advice. He said if I wanted to work with horses I should start by learning to shoe them. You learn everything there is to know about horses that way. So I became a blacksmith and worked cattle ranches for a while before I moved to a dude ranch," before adding wistfully, "because they had women and a social life. After that I got married but my wife found the life too remote. She wanted to talk to someone more than once a week when she went to the store." At this Sam looked a little bemused but I had to concede that she probably had a point. "Anyways we got in the car and drove south. Didn't have any plans about where we were going and didn't stop until we got to California. I got a job here at the Alisal and I've been here ever since."

Sam seemed to be perfectly happy living the life of a suburban cowboy. One of the reasons that Sam particularly liked working at the Alisal was that he played off six. He spent his weekends in his comfortable house in the "burbs", mowing the lawn in the mornings and taking his kids to little league soccer in the afternoons. And on weekdays, when his neighbours would be in their suits and ties and heading for the office, Sam would put on his duds and Stetson and drive to the ranch, where he would introduce dentists from Oakland and lawyers from Santa Monica to the wonders of horsemanship.

As the rest of the guests arrived Sam's expert eye flicked over each one of them in turn, sizing them up for their horsemanship simply by the way they walked and talked. Earlier I had told Sam that the last time I had been on a horse it was made of wood and it rocked. "Don't worry about it, Barrrrb, the horses go at walkin' pace here at the Alisal, single file head to toe, and you'll be followin' me," he said reassuringly.

A blackboard stood on the other side of the corral, nailed to the wall of the bunkhouse. It listed the names of the horses in alphabetical order. After Sam had done his sizing up of the paying customers, he went over to it and with a piece of chalk wrote down people's names next to the horses he had assigned to them. I strolled over there to check out my mount. The first thing I did was glance at the Ws just to make sure that old Sam hadn't put the greenhorn limey up on old Widowmaker. I'd seen that western. Instead I found my name scrawled up next to that of Concho, who, Sam assured me, was one of the most experienced and docile horses on the ranch. Next to the list of runners and riders was a map of the ranch. Blue and red lines snaked across it showing the routes of the different trail rides, like ski runs at Val D'Isere. How authentic the names were that dotted the map, I had no idea, but they certainly set the scene: Beaver Canyon Trail, Rawhide Road, Shaptaw Ridge and, most intriguing of all, Piss Ant Springs. I wondered if Sam and a couple of his wranglers had dreamed them up one night over a couple of bottles of Merlot in a Solvang eaterie.

Then Sam gave the order to mount up. The expression mounting up probably paints a picture of grabbing the pommel of the saddle, hooking a spurred boot into a stirrup and swinging the other leg in a smooth, lazy arc over the horse's back. But for me the Alisal provided the ignominy of a set of steps. As Sam had explained earlier, the horses never went faster than walking pace and followed one another nose to tail, so instead of setting off with a chorus of full throated "Yee-Hahs!", we opted for politely murmured "After yous" instead.

Sam led us out and the horses plodded one after the other nose to tail. I soon got the hang of it, rolling gently in the saddle to accommodate Concho's shambling gait. Sam led us off over the rolling hills of the ranch's 11,000 acres. The grass was gold in colour, made that way by the sun, and the scene reminded me of the Yorkshire Dales but with a perfect all-over tan. Before we set off Sam had given me some basic driving instructions, how to make Concho go, stop, turn left and right, that sort of thing. But I was more concerned with mastering the one hand holding the reins loosely and the other one resting nonchalantly mid thigh pose.

The sun was warm on my back, the rim of my hat (baseball) was pulled low over my eyes and I soon lulled myself into the idea that I had been born to the saddle. Two hours of clip-clopping later we plodded into a copse of trees to be greeted by the site of benches and two long tables laid out with red and white gingham tablecloths. Beside them stood a barbecue pit where strips of bacon, sausages and hunks of steak spat and sizzled. There were bubbling pots of beans, mashed potato, hash browns, corn cobs, biscuits, vats of gravy and jugs of freshly squeezed orange juice. And battered looking pots of coffee stood on the edge of the glowing coals wafting out their unmistakable mouth-watering aroma. We had arrived. One by one Sam led us up to another set of stairs on wheels, that had appeared out of nowhere, so the more geriatric amongst us we could dismount without putting out a hip. A couple of his wranglers led our mounts away for a well-earned nose bag of horse feed. Meanwhile we fell upon the food that had been prepared for us like an Apache raiding party. All I can say is that I ended my cowboy adventure on an authentic note, because the breakfast had come all the way from Dodge. Not Dodge City, but from the back of a Dodge four-wheel drive that had left the ranch half an hour before with all the food that had been cooked in the Alisal's gleaming kitchen.

It took me three days to drive to San Francisco, three glorious days of driving along a narrow road where cliffs and ridges clung to my right and the vast expanse of the Pacific Ocean stretched endlessly to my left, deep blue and dazzling with flecks of silver as the pale winter sunlight bounced off the ruffled waters. Just me, the open road and Cruise 103 playing Beach Boys hits on the radio for mile after mile after breathtaking mile. Big Sur, Morro Bay, San Luis Obispo, Carmel and Cannery Row made for short little detours, but the pull of the most beautiful highway in the world always proved too strong to make lingering anywhere much of an option.

San Francisco was big enough to be an exception though. I drove into San Francisco late in the evening and promptly drove straight out again. That's to say I drove straight through town without stopping to drive over the Golden Gate Bridge. There was a viewing area at the far end where I parked and got out and lent on the rail and took in the city as evening faded into night, the cityscape gradually turning from a fuzzy watercolour painting into an impressionistic work painted in neon.

The lure of San Francisco for me was summed up by the Scott McKenzie classic song *San Francisco*, the one that told us to wear some flowers in our hair. I had grown up with it and I still hear it played on radio stations to this day. On my first night I checked into a cheap hotel but next morning I went in search of some accommodation that was more in keeping. Ideally, I was looking for an Anna Madrigal style boarding house from *The Tales of the City* novels by Armistead Maupin, something with old-style architecture and peopled with an eclectic mix of characters. By chance I was lucky enough to find a small hotel that almost fitted the bill. The Hayes Valley Inn was more of a charming B&B, decked out in period style, and was run by Dennis, a very laid back San Franciscan. It was centrally located about 15 minutes walk from Union Square and the cable car stops, but best of all it was cheap. The defining characteristic of the place was that they welcomed dogs, and not just that but seemed to dote on them more than their guests.

Next day, with echoes of searching for the world of Suzie Wong in Hong Kong, I set off on foot to capture the spirit of the Summer of Love, when the hitherto quiet, stately looking, Victorian corner of San Francisco called Haight Ashbury became the worldwide headquarters of the hippy counterculture movement. Set against a contemporary backdrop of mom and pop conservatism, rampant consumerism and the Vietnam War approaching its zenith, the lure of plastering your Volkswagen van in psychedelic sunflowers and messages of peace and love and setting out from places like Des Moines, Iowa, and Topeka, Kansas, must have been all too much for a generation brought up on apple pie and Dr. Pepper.

First, over breakfast coffee, Dennis filled me in some of the background. "They say over 100,000 people came in 1967," he told me, "drawn by free food, free drugs and free love. But there's not much of it left now, just a few touristy shops and places selling nothing more mind changing than exotic tobacco."

It still proved a pleasant enough walk though. The houses were tall Victorian affairs, most of them were painted a uniform white but the occasional red, blue and purple ones added a dash of defiant colour. The hippy shops were long gone and had been replaced by boutiques and smart eateries, although a few lingered to attract the visitors. In fact, the Haight reminded me a lot of Brighton, on the south coast of England. A purple and green shop front with the name Dreams of Kathmandu caught my eye. Inside Tibetan prayer flags hung from the ceiling and the shelves were stacked with Buddha statues, Nepalese paper lanterns, batik work, ethnic jewellery and incense boxes, and signs told me that the owners took all the major credit cards. Still it was fun, but not as much fun as the Haight Ashbury T-shirts, which were floor to ceiling and wall to wall tie-dye.

Later, I walked past the Grateful Dead House at 710 Ashbury, a tall, narrow Victorian house which was painted pale purple and sported distinctly Gothic features, which made me think it looked like the kind of house the Adams Family might have retired to after they had given up scaring people for a living. Together with Janis Joplin and Jefferson Airplane, the Grateful Dead and their front man, Jerry Garcia, were the people I most associated with the Summer of Love, and it was one of the Grateful Dead band members who wrote the Scott McKenzie hit. But some of the ethos had survived, I noticed, as I walked past the Haight Ashbury Free Medical Clinic, which was set up in 1967, and was still dispensing free health care to the poor and needy of the area. How they had coped, I wondered, when the three letters that defined San Francisco in the sixties, LSD, became HIV, the scourge of the eighties. There were still a few hippies to be seen lounging in book stores or sipping coffee on street corners.

Were they originals who had been here in '67 and were simply still crazy after all these years, or were they just freeloaders who were panhandling and preying off tourists, it seemed rude to ask. That night back at the Hayes Valley Inn, Dennis told me how the dream had turned sour.

"It was just one glorious summer," he said, as if recalling the events placed him right back in the Summer of Love vernacular, "one beautiful, long, hot summer. But it didn't last. The drug dealers moved in and turf wars started, and the beautiful children left and went home or back to college to learn how to become lawyers and bankers." There's no doubt in my mind though that something very special happened in Haight Ashbury back in 1967, something that was hedonistic certainly and naively full of promise. Having walked its now gentrified streets, and recalling a lyric or two from Scott Mackenzie's defining classic, I'd been able I felt to get a hint of what *"turning on, tuning in and dropping out"* during the Summer of Love might have been about, like catching a faint whiff of marijuana on the breeze. "Do you know what his real name was?" asked Dennis. "Who?" I replied. "Scott Mackenzie, it was Phillip Wallach Blondheim, and he was from Jacksonville, Florida." Even so I was glad I had been to San Francisco, even if I hadn't worn some flowers in my hair.

The Pacific Coast Highway had given me a taste for the open road. The only problem was I needed a destination, somewhere to aim for. Alison was an old friend. She was Australian and I first met her ten years ago when she was seeing Europe and working in a pub in St. John's Wood. While she was working there she had met an American marine and he had married her and carted her off to live with him in the States. They had moved around a lot, from base to base, and we had lost touch. Then out of the blue she e-mailed me saying that she was now living in Longmont, a small town near Denver, Colorado. Her husband was no longer in the picture and she was planning to return to Australia in the near future. She had heard that I was travelling, so she had got in touch to say that if I happened to be passing it would be great to see me. A quick look at my road map told me that from San Francisco I could drive to Denver via Yosemite National Park, Death Valley, Las Vegas, the Grand Canyon and Monument Valley before crossing the Rockies and dropping down into the city. I gave myself ten days to make the trip, said farewell to San Francisco and hit the road.

Some of the early American landscape painters who captured Yosemite on canvas were inspired by its natural beauty and epic scale to portray it as the Garden of Eden. Driving through the Yosemite Valley it was easy to see why. The sheer rock faces of El Capitan and Half Dome rose thousands of feet straight up from the valley floor which was carpeted with ancient sequoias and wild flowers, and was further spotted with mountain lakes that sparkled in the sunshine and which were fed by sweeping rivers and plunging waterfalls with names like Bridalveil. Later the views were softened by forests of tall, pointing spruce and pine that shimmered in undulating shades of deep emerald. At the visitor centre I paid the attendant my $20 fee and asked her what was the best way to drive to Death Valley. She recommended I head south towards Bakersfield, and spent the rest of the morning driving along the snaking roads that wound across the valley floor and up on to pine clad ridges, stopping frequently to walk up to where a waterfall fell 500 feet into a black mountain pool, or just to wind down the window and feel the cold air on my face and listen to the silence.

The road that led from the park to Bakersfield was a three-lane highway. Juggernauts thundered past me in the fast lane for three hours, and I was anticipating more of the same when just outside Bakersfield my map told me to take Highway 178. Within minutes of taking the turn-off I joined a two-lane blacktop that snaked through mile after mile of canyons hugging the bank of a narrow rock-strewn river. Every quarter mile or so a turn in the road would reveal a view of a rugged ridge of red sandstone against the cobalt blue of a cloudless sky, each one more dramatic than the last. The road climbed as it twisted and turned, and leaving the river below I emerged onto a plateau surrounded by jagged peaks in the distance. At Lake Isabella I stopped to fill up with gas, and in the gas station shop bought a packet of biscuits and a large bottle of Coke as a late lunch. The town was small, numbering a couple of hundred houses and assorted stores so there was nothing to keep me there. I drove on and stopped at a parking spot overlooking the lake and watched a windsurfer hurtle across the surface at a good clip. I didn't linger long as my plan was to drive into Death Valley before nightfall, find somewhere to stay, and be ready to explore the valley first thing in the morning. Later that evening, I crossed the Sierras as the sun set on the horizon daubing the evening sky with hues of blues, pink, and orange.

"Stovepipe Wells gets its name from the early settlers who hammered a stovepipe into the ground to mark where the only source of water to be found here was," said Ron as he swilled the beer in his glass on the heavy wood bar top. "You took a real chance not booking somewhere to stay before driving into the valley," he told me, "even it being outta season you were taking a helluva chance. You wouldn't wanna be spending a night in that little car of yours, that's for sure." Ron, I soon learnt, was something of an expert on Death Valley. An hour earlier I had driven up to the Stovepipe Wells Hotel which was a two storey affair of scattered rooms arranged round a central reception area, and which stood on the valley floor surrounded by mesquite flats and sand dunes.

Ron was a big guy with a bushy, twirly moustache that made him look like the bad guy in the silent movies who was always chaining Pearl Bailey to the railway tracks. We got chatting over a beer or two in the hotel bar and it transpired he lived in Reno across the state line in Nevada. All day long he drove a truck for a living. And then as soon as the weekend came along he liked to relax by getting into his RV and driving for hours to get to Death Valley. Then when he got here he drove around it for up to ten hours a day. It wasn't that Ron was an obsessive driver, he just couldn't leave the place alone. It exerted a messianic pull on him. The next morning I found out why. It was a bright, cold, clear-sky day and the valley was lit majestically. Death Valley has to be one of the most desolate wildernesses on the planet, and was shaped by geological events that started five hundred million years ago. I drove for miles across the valley floor, a sea of crusted salt flats, with islands of colour showing where various different mineral deposits had been exposed. For many thousands of years the actions of long dead rivers and the constant wind had etched and furrowed the bare rock into intricate patterns. Man, in his own very small way, had made his small scratch on the surface as well. In the 1860s Death Valley experienced a mini mining boom and pioneers braved the searing heat and arid dryness to scrape for gold, silver, copper and lead. I spotted evidence of this driving past a road sign that pointed down a dusty track that was called Twenty Mule Train Canyon. It was just one of the evocative names that echoed the valley's past. The others included Furnace Creek, Daylight Pass, Golden Canyon, Mesquite Flats, Devils Cornfield, Dante's Peak, Saline Valley, Badwater and the ghost town of Skidoo.

I drove into Las Vegas late in the evening and drove straight to a visitor centre where the girl behind the counter got on the phone and found me a room at the Frontier Hotel and Casino at the less glamorous end of the strip. This suited me fine. Driving along the strip, Vegas reminded me of a beauty pageant. At one end of the line were the shiny, new themed hotels: Luxor, New York, New York and Bellagio. They were the new kids on the block; young and beautiful, they had all the latest gimmicks with which to tempt the tourists. Down at the other end were the faded beauties, the casino hotels that had made Las Vegas in the fifties a byword for style, when Sammy Davis, Dean Martin, Peter Lawford, Joey Bishop, and the chairman of the board himself, Mr. Frank Sinatra, called the shots and made the desert oasis the capital of cool.

The Frontier was just across the street from Flamingos, one of the old survivors whose name, I was delighted to see, was still displayed with the most spectacular neon sign on the strip. For me these older hotel casinos were the stuff of legend. They were the ones that had put Vegas on the map. The upper end of the strip was where the hotels were more like indoor theme parks, where twice a day Friedrich and Roy would make their brace of performing white tigers jump through hoops of fire, and massive billboards announced that the magician, David Copperfield, would make an elephant disappear before your eyes live on stage. All Frank needed to keep an audience enthralled was to be spot-lit on an empty stage wearing a snap brim hat, holding a cigarette in one hand and a microphone in the other, while he sang a hit song backed up by a Nelson Riddle arrangement. Vegas felt like arriving at a nightclub only to be told you should have been here the night before, when they'd had a real wild party.

I soon discovered that one of the great things about modern day Vegas though is that it's one of the few places in America where you'll meet Americans from all over America. Three quarters of Americans don't own a passport, and a massively high number of Americans have never been out of their home state. But those that do travel on their precious two weeks annual vacation, a large number of them anyway, head for Las Vegas. So a row of slot machines in a Las Vegas casino can be a lot like the Stars and Stripes. Each butt on a stool feeding the slot machines was like a star on the flag. Dressed in plaid shirts, jeans, training shoes and baseball caps emblazoned with the names of various agricultural dry-feed manufacturers, they all looked identical but represented a multitude of different states, as they stared straight ahead of them transfixed by the tumbling symbols before their dulled eyes. Or maybe the entire resort had been taken over by a particularly large party from Indiana, it was hard to tell.

If there was little to tell the punters apart, at least the hotel casinos went to great lengths to give themselves distinct identities. From the outside New York, New York was a panorama of the Manhattan skyline, complete with a rollercoaster that snaked round the Empire State Building and over the Statue of Liberty. Luxor was a huge black vinyl pyramid ten stories high. The fact that there aren't any pyramids at Luxor seemed to have escaped the architect who designed it, but what the hell, Vegas was supposed to be a fun town not a history lesson. And Excalibur was an Arthurian legend castle straight out of Disney with lots of towers, streaming pennants and knights on horseback. No matter how hard they tried to establish their individual themes on the outside, once inside they quickly began to look a lot alike. The acres of slots were laid out in the same fashion wherever you went. The blackjack tables always seemed to be next to the craps tables which were always to be found at right-angles across from the roulette tables, and so forth. What added to the sense of uniformity was the curious music made by the sound of the constant chug and ping of thousands of slot machines being played simultaneously, the constant click of chips and the monotone, rat-a-tat-tat, verbal delivery of the croupiers as they invited people to place their bets.

For those Americans who are prepared to travel though, the ultimate vacation destination is Europe. And for those who aren't, Las Vegas had brought Europe to them in the shape of the Venetian and Paris hotel casinos. The Venetian boasted a replica Doge's Palace, replica Campanile in St Mark's Square, replica Rialto Bridge and replica gondola rides with replica gondoliers serenading romantic couples with *O Sole Mio*. They probably sang Country and Western ballads in the evenings at some replica Nashville hillbilly bar somewhere else on the strip. The gondoliers didn't even have to do that fancy figure of eight swizzle thing with the oar at the back either, because all the boats were fixed to an underwater track that dragged them along at a respectable pace, like a slowed down log flume at a theme park only without the big splash at the end. This was where you could slowly explore the "Grand Canal". But instead of drifting by palazzos and churches it was lined with shops selling all kinds of expensive jewellery and fashions, and these new merchants of Venice had names like Bulgari, Swarovski and Armani.

I had always thought that America had four time zones. I soon realised that there's a fifth, and it's one that most people don't know about, the Las Vegas time zone. Actually, time in Las Vegas turned out to be a bit of a misnomer because, in a way, time didn't exist, not in a connected to the rest of the world sense anyway. Sunrise and sunset didn't have much of a bearing in Vegas, because reminding people that it's time to go to bed isn't good for business. So inside the casinos it was daytime all the time. I could see how they got away with it too. The geography certainly helped. Las Vegas is situated in the heart of a very hot and very dry desert. So naturally nobody goes outside unless they can possibly avoid it. This tended to create a highly artificial way of living and you could quite easily spend an entire week inside your hotel casino and never venture outside at all. Inside it was comfortably air-conditioned twenty-four hours a day, the lights were on all the time, and the action never stopped. This must be great for visitors from abroad, I thought, as I strolled through one of the crowded casinos that was still going full pelt at two o'clock in the morning. There would be no jet lag because you could simply bring your home time zone with you, live by your normal waking and sleeping hours, and never have to adjust your body clock.

The Desert Inn and The Sands, with its famous Copa Room which the Brat Pack made their own, and which sacrilegiously was bulldozed to make way for The Venetian, may have been long gone, but one of the grand dames still remained. I entered Caesar's Palace on a travelator that was modelled on what I guessed was the Appian Way. Without having to put one foot in front of the other, I silently glided past a procession of marble statues of the great and the good of ancient Rome. Inside, the shopping mall was designed as a square in the eternal city and the gods of the fashion world were well represented. Each one had its own temple dedicated to itself: Emporio Armani, Versace, Fendi, DKNY and Abercrombie and Fitch. Shoppers, like gladiators, threw themselves on their mercy, brandishing their credit cards while mouthing silently, "Those who are about to buy, salute you". The boutiques were arranged down both sides of boulevards that ran from a central courtyard that was dominated by a huge fountain. The centrepiece was an explosion of marble statuary and cascading water. It depicted Roman gods, conquering heroes and rearing winged horses: manes flew, nostrils flared and marble muscles bulged. They burst out of a landslide of falling rocks and torrents of water gushed out from all around them, and the entire scene was half encircled by a broken colonnade of marble columns. It was a popular spot for visitors to take photos and flashed constantly flashed. I wondered if this fountain wasn't more photographed than the Trevi one in Rome. The sky above it was lit in such a way that it went through the equivalent of a twenty-four hour cycle every three hours, which must have made it the only place in Vegas that acknowledged that some semblance of normal time existed elsewhere on the planet. But for all its over the top posturing, Caesar's still managed to retain a semblance of the old Las Vegas, before everything became pastiches of other places. Not far away from the fountain stood a replica of Michelangelo's David. It stood eighteen feet tall and, I was told, was sculpted from a slab of marble hewn from the same quarry as the original.

In the Café Roma my waitress picked up on my accent and asked me where I lived. "London," I replied. "Oh, I used to live just off Park Lane," she told me as she topped up my coffee cup. She was American, and I wondered how you went from living off Park Lane to serving coffee in a Las Vegas restaurant. "Oh, I was married to a wealthy man," she said as if reading my thoughts. "But I prefer to be a free woman, even if it means working here." I thought she must have been the only American in the world to get a duff divorce lawyer. Otherwise how could she have failed to get her hands on a sizeable lump of disposable income from a man who could afford to buy property on the second most expensive square on the Monopoly board. But then again this was Las Vegas so maybe she had arrived with a sizeable stash and gambled it all away. When I paid my check she brought me my change, which was a pile of quarters for the slots.

The hooker was a rare sight in Vegas. I was standing at a traffic junction waiting for the lights to change to cross the road back to my hotel.

She was negotiating with three guys. Ladies of the night were seldom seen out in public. Las Vegas may have had a sleazy reputation in the past but business had shifted more towards family holidays in recent years, and that meant Las Vegas needed a clean-cut image if Disney and Florida weren't going to get everything their own way. But this being Vegas meant you couldn't keep a good man-eater down. Hookers were still to be found on the streets, but not standing under street lamps, instead they advertised their wares in special edition magazines that were stacked in vending machines and dotted along the pavement up and down the strip at regular intervals. They were glossy, smooth to the touch and decked out in lurid colours. I'm talking about the magazines, not the girls. And they were filled with pictures of women posing provocatively above phone numbers. Euphemistically, all the ads said that the women were available to come to your room for a private dancing session. A few of the ads bore a label saying "Actual Photo", so chances were in the main what you saw in the ad wasn't what you got. But the hooker at the crossroads was the only one I saw in the flesh and she wasn't dressed like a dancer. She wore a bright red bra top which revealed a swathe of bare midriff, a black leather micro miniskirt and knee-high black boots. The negotiation was going on fast and furiously. Finally, she clinched the deal saying, "OK guys, that's a hundred bucks for the room for an hour and 75 bucks each." There was a short pause and then she added, "Oh, and I'll take you to paradise." At this the guys all visibly perked up, but I think she was referring to the name of a cheap hotel off the Strip.

My road map told me there was very little between Las Vegas and Denver in terms of major cities. What did lie ahead, of course, was some of the most awe inspiring natural wilderness to be found anywhere, which began with the Grand Canyon. It's one of America's great ironies that they chose to build Las Vegas, a town dedicated to replicating places like

Paris and Venice, in the back yard of the greatest wonder of the natural world. I arrived in the late afternoon at one of the handful of designated viewing place on the south rim. I parked the car and saw a hundred yards ahead of me groups of visitors all with their backs to me. They stood in huddles looking out into the distance. This is one of the more dramatic aspects of the Grand Canyon, unlike mountain ranges or waterfalls that you can see from a distance as you approach, the Grand Canyon is almost completely invisible until you're upon it. I threaded my way through the trees to the paved viewing platform which snaked a couple of hundred yards in both directions, and was flanked by a low knee-high wall. And there it was. There are no words to describe the Grand Canyon so here are the facts. The Grand Canyon is 227 miles long, up to 18 miles wide and up to one mile deep. For well over an hour I just stood and stared. What the facts don't tell you about are the myriad layers of rainbow strata that reveal the earth's geology over millions of years, and how they radiate shimmering colours the clouds throw dappled patches of shade over them. My gaze followed the thin snaking line of the Colorado river a mile below my feet and I wondered how was it possible for that thread of blue to have carved all this. I struggled to sear every detail, colour, shadow ridge, plunge and jutting escarpment outcrop into my memory, knowing full well that such an effort was completely futile and that what I was looking at would at best only ever return to my memory as a feint outline and impression, and which would stay with me to my last day. I still try to recapture that hour-long moment in my mind's eye and sometimes vivid hints of it pop into my head unexpectedly, and my brain reels as it struggles to recapture the whole image for a fleeting second or two, putting together visual scraps like a child with a join the dots picture book. I'm convinced that the first unwitting pioneer who stumbled across the Grand Canyon experienced a moment that was more profound than when Neil Armstrong set foot on the moon.

~

I knew of Monument Valley from John Ford westerns. Its sandstone buttes, dramatically shaped by the wind and which stand a thousand feet above the surrounding sandy plain have become the visual icon of the Wild West. The film director John Ford, who did more to immortalise Monument Valley on celluloid than anyone else, called it, "the most complete, beautiful and peaceful place on earth." For thousands of years Monument Valley has been the ancestral homeland of the Najavo nation, its name simply translates as "Valley of the Rocks".

It was dark as I approached Monument Valley so I deliberately overshot it and drove on to the town with the crackerjack name of Mexican Hat to find a motel for the night. I arrived at about eight o'clock, found a place, checked in, took a shower and emerged about 8.30 looking for perhaps a place to have a beer and then find something to eat. Mexican Hat was a one street town and when I stepped out of my door right on to the street it was completely dark. The whole town had gone to bed. Nowhere was open, so I got back in the car and drove about five miles to a petrol station I had passed on the way in and dined on microwave food and a soft drink. I was back less than an hour later and there was nothing else to do but get an early night. Just as well as the next morning dawned bright and sunny and I was keen to drive into the valley. I drove along Highway 163 across a flat plain of desert ahead of me. Battered looking caravans dotted the landscape, most of them with a rusting old Ford or pick-up parked outside. These were the homes of Navajo people who looked like they were desperately trying to cling to a bygone way of life. Highway 163 ran straight as an arrow towards a cleft in the imposing massif that lay ahead. A turn-off led into the valley and suddenly, as if a curtain had been pulled aside, I found myself driving onto a vast plain that stretched to a distant horizon. Giant mesas and buttes of red sandstone, some of which towered a thousand feet above the sandy plain, the result of millions of years of wind sculpting.

At the visitor centre I paid my $15 and in return was given a map of the Valley Drive. I slid back behind the wheel and my little Ford compact bounced and slithered in the loose gravel and dust as I steered it for three hours around the breathtaking slalom course of towering mesas and buttes. In one way it felt no less spectacular than the Grand Canyon. What they both possessed in equal measure was scale, but Monument Valley slightly edged it in atmosphere. There was something uniquely haunting about the landscape, and because you could drive and get out and walk around it, it felt emotionally more accessible. Back at the visitor centre I spent an hour in the small museum that detailed the history of Najavo life in the valley. Surely, to have lived in such a place they must have felt that they were a chosen people. Driving out past the isolated trailers and caravans I wondered how the Navajo who still chose to live there could stand the sense of loss of what must have been a truly remarkable way of life.

Three days later I drove into Denver. Mind you, I very nearly didn't get there. Somewhat stupidly, when I hired my car in LA and bought a road map, I'd forgotten that road maps don't generally show topography, and there was one rather large obstacle between me and the mile high city of Denver, namely the Rocky Mountains. You have to remember I was driving a Ford compact that housewives use to go to the mall to do their shopping in the suburbs. As I climbed ever higher towards the apex of the 14,000 feet high range, passing signposts for Vail and other up-market ski resorts, heavy snow carpeted the road and swirled in gusts plastering my windscreen in big, white soggy flakes that the wipers smeared across my view. And every time a heavy truck or four-wheel-drive overtook me it threw handfuls of grit at my windscreen. My little car quickly became uncontrollable as with no grip it constantly slithered across the road like a puck on an ice rink, the wheels racing for purchase as I drifted towards the towering wheels of heavy duty trucks that thundered past me on either side. There was no turning off the highway, and no turning back. As night fell the snow began to fall in ever thicker flurries, reducing visibility to a few yards, and still the lorries and heavy goods vehicles ground past me one after the other so that I felt I was trapped in a narrow canyon of heavy moving metal. The only thing to do was every time a four-wheel drive overtook me I hit the gas and tried to stay in its tyre tracks for as long as possible. But inevitably each one would steadily creep away from me and leave me in a slithering white fog, praying for the tell-tale rear lights of another one to pull in front of me and give me a precious couple of hundred yards of easier driving in its tracks before it too pulled away. Illuminated road signs arched over the highway flashing warning signs to the motorists below and at regular intervals I would be harangued repeatedly in neon to…STOP AND FIX SNOW CHAINS. Snow chains? I had a sun roof. Four hours of cat and mouse driving later a sign for Denver Airport appeared and I peeled off and followed it all the way to the car rental depot where Alison was there to meet me.

I spent a couple of days catching up with Alison and generally getting my heart rate back to normal after my Rocky Mountains driving ordeal. Longmont, where she lived, was a small pleasant little town about half an hour's drive from its cooler neighbour, Boulder. Located in the heart of a natural wilderness, there was a distinctly outdoorsy feeling about Boulder, which is also home to the University of Colorado and attracts students from all over the USA, giving the town a young and energetic vibe. It also has a thriving Arts scene and a number of internet businesses and creative start ups had chosen to set up shop there. This all contributed to giving Boulder an almost cosmopolitan atmosphere. Strolling around the downtown area we passed funky little shops, boutiques selling native American crafts and elegant book store cafes. It was like a little corner of

Santa Barbara had got bored with the beach, upped sticks and moved to the mountains.

"Let's go for afternoon tea," said Alison. "Love to," I said, and meant it after two weeks of truck stop coffee on the interstates and highways had left me with a tongue that felt like a dirty carpet. "Do they do tea in Boulder," I asked, enunciating the word tea with a Bertie Wooster style hint of hauteur. It crossed my mind to mention that the last time I had enjoyed proper afternoon tea had been in the Windamere in Darjeeling, and that I very much suspected that cowboy country Colorado wasn't going to be able to get anywhere near to matching the experience. "Well, we've got one place that's a little bit different," said Alison with a smile.

Okay, hands up if you can point to Tajikistan on a map of the world. I couldn't then and I still can't now, but it feels like I've been there, and that's all thanks to the Dushanbe Tea House, which Alison took me to, and stands between the bubbling Boulder creek and the Boulder Museum of Contemporary Art. A pergola arched overhead as we approached the traditionally built Tea House which was adorned on the outside with eight magnificent ceramic panels that depicted the Tree of Life, and looked as if they had been raided from a palace somewhere along the Silk Road. As we stepped inside everything about the interior fought for our attention. Twelve intricately carved cedar columns supported a hand-painted ceiling of intricate colour and design, and in front of us stood a tableau of copper statues depicting characters from a traditional poem. Beyond them the elegant room was laid out with tables, bedecked in crisp, white linen, where huddles of Boulder's finest were sitting chatting quietly. Taco Bell, it wasn't. We were shown to a table and we ordered high tea, which, when it arrived, was a three tier tower of scones, jams, cream and cakes to rival anything served in Fortnum & Mason on Piccadilly.

"Quite a place, isn't it," said Alison, "it's a gift from the people of the town of Dushanbe in Tajikistan, which has been twinned with Boulder.

It was built by forty artisans over there, all by hand, and then broken down and shipped out here to be reconstructed."

"Did they get anything in return," I asked.

"Oh sure," said Alison, "we gave them a cyber café." Even though I didn't know where Tajikistan was, I had an image of some far-flung, run down, former enclave of the Soviet Union, and I wasn't at all sure they had got the best of the bargain. In fact, if I had been one of the good citizens of Boulder, I would have felt extremely embarrassed at being the recipient of such cultural largesse in return for something that sounded like it consisted mainly of Formica and computer terminals.

I would have liked to have lingered longer in Boulder but for once I was on something of a schedule. Back in the UK when I was planning my trip I had heard about a man called John Ruskey. He ran a small business taking small groups of people and individuals out on the Mississippi river in a canoe for days at a time, camping overnight on islands in the river and deserted sandbars. I had come to Mark Twain's *Huckleberry Finn* somewhat late in life but loved the book all the same, and going down that Old Man River in a canoe sounded like an adventure ripped straight from its pages.

SEVEN

Mississippi Yearning

I got a hint of the Old South before I had even set eyes on the river when I checked into the Shack Up Inn. This most individual of hotels was sited on the old Hopson Plantation just outside Clarksdale in the state of Mississippi. What made it unique were the rooms, which were converted shotgun shacks. The place was run by Guy and Bill and Bill led me over to the dilapidated looking dwelling which lay across the lawn from the reception area and restaurant. "A lot of people think shotgun shacks are where slaves lived in the old days," he explained, "but that's not true. They're old sharecropper's houses. Anyway, we've put you in the Robert Clay shack."

The building we approached looked like it had been modelled on a railway carriage. It had rough wood walls and a tin roof with a chimney stack. It stood a couple of feet off the ground and was fronted by a wooden porch, complete with rocking chair. It wasn't hard to imagine some old hillbilly grandmother sitting there, puffing on a pipe and with a shotgun across her knees. Bill led me inside explaining the layout. "Shotgun shacks get their name," explained Bill, "because of the way they're built. They're both short and narrow and they're made up of three rooms running one behind the other, the living room, bedroom and kitchen. They don't have connecting corridors, just a door in the same position in each room. So when all the doors are open they said you could fire a shotgun into the house at the front and the bullet would fly out at the back without hitting anything." The untreated wooden planks of the porch squeaked as he led me across them and into the front room. "It's an original shack," said Bill as we stepped into the dark gloomy interior. He flicked the light switch on the wall and the interior was lit with a warm glow that illuminated a cosy living room that was dominated by a wooden breakfast bar at one end and a small piano at the other. A faded rug covered most of the strip wood floor on which stood a couple of small sofas and the walls were lined with period mirrors and prints depicting life on the plantation from years gone by. "We've put in all the modern conveniences," said Bill, "but kept the old ambience of the place."

This was more in evidence in the kitchen which boasted a microwave, a refrigerator and a cooking range. They'd also plumbed in a modern bathroom. "In the old days, they had to make do with an outhouse," said Bill. The place absolutely reeked of authentic atmosphere. "This used to be old Robert Clay's shack," Bill said, "he was a black sharecropper and he raised seven kids here all on his own. He did a pretty good job too. They all went to college and made something of themselves. Towards the end they tried to move old Robert into a nice place in town but he didn't want to move. He died in this here shack." The shacks were clearly a labour of love and Bill went on to explain that they had 14 of them spread around the property and that they were all originals and came from nearby plantations. "These walls," he said as he stroked one of them lovingly, "are made from cedar wood grown on the plantation. It's the same story with all of them."

Later that evening, over a beer with Bill, he told me that the idea behind the Shack Up Inn was to preserve a little piece of Southern history. He also filled me in on Clarksdale. "It's the home of the Delta Blues," he told me, "but John can tell you more about that than I can. He used to run the place." John was John Ruskey, the man I would be meeting tomorrow morning and would be taking me on the river for five days. "He called for you by the way, and said to meet him at Quapaw."

"Where's that?" I asked.

"That's his place where he keeps the canoes, but don't worry I'll give you directions in the morning."

That night as I hunkered down in the old shack where Robert Clay had raised seven sons without running water or electricity, I wondered what he would have thought of his old house, where he had been trapped in sharecropper poverty, being turned into a tourist trap for the wealthy who could indulge themselves by attempting to recapture a hint of the Old South. At the very least, I hoped that he would raise his hat to me for braving the mighty Mississippi river. Not many tourists who stayed in his old shack did that.

When I eventually found John Ruskey's place it was in a compound on the edge of Clarksdale. The Quapaw Canoe Company was housed on the ground floor of a three storey building cut into the banks of the Sunflower River. As I pulled into the yard a man emerged from a battered doorway and strolled over to my car. He was dressed in frayed jeans and a sleeveless denim shirt. He also wore a crumbled brim straw hat and his feet were bare. He looked like he had stepped right out of a poster for Jack Daniels. Deep brown, intelligent, lively eyes summed me up in a moment.

"Hi there, Bob," John Ruskey drawled the words in such a lazy way they seemed to drip off the end of his chin as they came out of his mouth. When he extended his arm to shake my hand his bicep bunched up like a baseball, no doubt the result of many hard years of paddling on the Mississippi.

"Thanks John, it's great to be here, sorry I'm late but I had a little trouble finding you."

"Don't worry about it Bob," said John, "you're on river time now. That's Wesley," he said introducing a huge black man. "He'll be driving us and the gear to the river once we load up." Wesley ambled over and took my hand in his giant paw. "Hi there," he said, and his voice rumbled like quiet thunder. An old, battered Chevy truck stood in the yard surrounded by mounds of gear and a nine feet long metal canoe. The gear included a two man tent, two large cool boxes, a five gallon water drum, cooking gear, a medical kit, a walkie-talkie, life jackets and a couple of long wooden paddles. "Everything we're gonna need, we have to take with us," said John, "there are no five and dimes where we're going." Then John produced what looked like a heavy duty oilskin duffel bag. "You don't need many clothes for the river," he said, "let's sort out what you need and you can leave the rest here." Together we sorted through my suitcase which looked very out of place and basically selected two of everything I'd need, and I'd already been pre-warned to bring a large hat. Next John showed me how to pack all my personal stuff into the waterproof duffel bag and secure it. "Even if we end up in the river, they should stay dry," he said, "not that that's the general idea," he added with a grin. It didn't take us more than five minutes to stow all the gear onto the flat bed of the truck. "OK, let's get going," said John.

Wesley drove and we sat three abreast across the front seat of the big truck. The radio was tuned to a local station and filled the cab with the strains of Delta Blues. "We'll spend four nights on the river, Bob," John explained. "We'll be heading down river but the river's kind of windy down here so we won't end up further than 50 miles from where we are now, that how you figure it Wes?" A rumbling growl from my immediate left announced Wesley's agreement. "Pull in up there ahead Wes," said John pointing through the bug spattered windscreen at a service station in the dusty distance. As Wes drew up John said, "There's a shop inside Bob if you want to load up with any last minute supplies, and there's still plenty of room in one of the cool boxes for a stash of beers." I took the hint and hopped out and bought four six-packs figuring that a hard day's paddling should do wonders for building up a decent thirst.

Wesley hauled on the steering wheel and the big old truck slid off the main road onto the first of a series of gravel winding roads that took us on a twisting path over the levee and through copses of woods. Then we pulled up in a shady clearing where a pebbly beach ran down to the edge of the river. I hopped out after John and stretched my legs. It was just after lunchtime and the sun shone out of a clear sky where only a few wispy clouds drifted in the breeze throwing their shadows like grey follow spotlights onto the landscape. I walked down through the trees and took in my first view of the mighty Mississippi. The one thing you have to keep reminding yourself about the Mississippi is that it's a river. What I was standing beside would have dwarfed Lake Windermere or Conniston. An inland sea stretched ahead of me and I wasn't looking down the river, I was looking directly across it. It was muddy brown and a strong wind was whipping it up into white-topped waves where it blew counter to the currents and eddies that coursed just beneath its surface. Suddenly, John's nine feet canoe was looking very puny indeed.

"So what are ya thinking, Bob?" John had materialised beside me. How long he'd been there I couldn't tell but I got the distinct impression that John hadn't wanted to disturb the moment. Everyone's first sighting of the Mississippi is a special moment and there was something of the mystical about John, I was already beginning to realise, when it came to the river.

"Bloody hell, it's big isn't it," I said.

"Fourth largest river in the world," he said, "and she's over 2,500 miles long. The Missouri River joins her at Saint Louis. She's known as "the Big Muddy" which is why the Mississippi is that dark colour in the lower reaches. They say down here that if you drink river water you can grow corn in your stomach."

I gazed across at the far bank in the distance. "How far is it to the opposite bank" I asked John, pointing at the distant line of thick green vegetation.

"That's over a mile," he said. He paused while I let the enormity of a mile wide river sink in. "But that's not the far bank, it's a river island.

They'll be another mile or so of river on the other side before you get to the opposite bank."

"Are you telling me the Mississippi is over two miles wide," I asked incredulously.

"Sure," said John, "but she's over ten miles wide in some stretches. We're in the Delta now so she takes things pretty slow. Down here she flows at about half your natural walking speed. But there's a lotta water behind her so you don't want to get caught in the current. If you do she won't let you go. So if you want to go for a swim stick with me, I know the safe places."

We unloaded all the gear from the truck and John expertly managed to pack it all into our nine feet canoe. It left a small island of space for him at the back, and a similar one for me at the front that I could just about squeeze myself into. Having arranged all the gear John then stripped off his shirt and walked out into the river and plunged below the surface. He emerged moments later with a beatific look on his face and shook diamond beads of water from his beard as he shook his head. Suddenly, I was transported back to dawn on the Ganges at Varanasi. John seemed to share the same sense of spirituality the *sadhus* had displayed. I didn't take it as a challenge, but I thought if I'm going to spends five days in a canoe, and a two man tent, with this man in this vast watery wilderness, it would probably be a good idea if I demonstrated a sense of comradeship. So not to be outdone I also stripped off my shirt and waded in after him. The water was surprisingly warm, or at least not cold, and slipping below the surface of the mighty river, and to be in its grip, be it only the lightest brush of its fingertips, truly possessed something of an epiphany moment, with the spirit of Huckleberry Finn serving as my John the Baptist.

That first afternoon the going was pretty easy despite my having to use muscles that had hardly ever been used before. I had never set foot in a canoe before and the first thing to master was acquiring the necessary sense of balance. The wind was at our backs but as we cleared the first bend, the wind shifted to come at us from out of the east; whipping the surface of the river into choppy waves. We dug in hard for a good hour, quickly finding a steady rhythm with our paddling.

John soon gave me a couple of tips on technique, so that each time I lifted my paddle out of the water I didn't deposit a cupful of water into his lap. "Just give the handle of the paddle a little twist so that the blade flicks away from the canoe when it leaves the water," he said. Me being a first-timer, John had planned to take things easy that first afternoon and within a couple of hours he steered us on to a sandy beach on a deserted sandbar island. As we approached, dipping our paddles in happy unison now into the choppy waters of the river, John gave me a quick rundown on what to look out for in a good campsite: "Good access, so you don't have to carry the gear too far from the canoe," he said. "Plenty of driftwood for the fire. Trees for shade and shelter from the wind, and most important of all," he paused, his eyes narrowed and scanned the island for telltale signs that were clearly lost on me, "It's gotta look kinda nice," he added with a broad grin.

Setting up camp that first night on the river became something of a ritual that would be repeated over the next few days. We paddled hard the last few strokes to put on a spurt to help us beach the canoe. As the bow bit into the soft sand, John hopped out and I quickly followed him, and together we dragged the canoe a few feet up on to the beach. Together, we unloaded all the gear. The first job was always to erect the tent, which was a lot easier when it was a two-man job, then John dispatched me to find driftwood for a fire while he arranged the camp. It took me the best part of an hour to find and haul dry lumps of driftwood that I found along the shoreline. By the time I had dropped the last bits on a pile that John said was enough, I was ravenous. I also saw that John had unloaded the cool box with the beers and was looking forward to blowing the froth off one as the Australians say, when John gave me a final task. "Take this, Bob," he said, handing me what looked like a cross between a bushman's knife and a machete, and which sported a wicked looking serrated blade about 18 inches long. "You can use it," John said, "for sawing off thin branches. What I want you to do," he added, "is cut me a bunch of willow branches about two feet long and as thick as your finger. I'll put them over the fire and we'll have willow smoked steaks for dinner." John pointed out what were willows and what weren't and I wandered off and started harvesting small branches; chopping, hacking and sawing until my arm got too sore to do any more.

When I got back to camp, John had it all laid out with military precision centred round a roaring fire. "They're fine," he said as he took the willow branches from my arms. "Let's have a swim and then I reckon you could do with a cold beer." Our section of beach formed a gently curving bay which John said would make it safe for us to swim if we didn't venture out more than a few feet. I followed and my feet were sucked into loamy sand and muck that squelched through my toes. Even in our sheltered bay, the outer fringes of the slowly moving current of the mighty river pulled at our bodies with frightening force. A few yards downriver a large tree had fallen into the water and jutted out at a right angle. Not all of its gnarled limbs were fully submerged and it had left a driftwood trellis of sun bleached branches sticking above the surface of the water. "Follow me," said John, "this is a bit of nature's luxury I think you're going to enjoy." He was standing waist high in the water and turned and slowly lowered himself until he was fully immersed in the water. He let the current carry him down towards the fallen tree. Gingerly, I followed his lead. John drifted down to the tree and turned so that he was facing back towards the current. He found a branch to sit on with the trunk of the tree supporting his back. "Find a branch to sit on, Bob," he called out, "and then just lean back into the tree." I found a suitable branch and turned back to face the current which swirled around me pulling at my flesh while pinning me to the bole of the trunk of the tree. "Your first Mississippi Jacuzzi," said John, "and the river gives you a massage at the same time." After a hard day's paddling it was the perfect treatment for my aching muscles. Half an hour later it was the sound of John topping a couple of cold beers that he'd taken from the cool box that finally broke the spell and propelled me out of the river's soothing embrace.

Before we had entered the water John had put the steaks to cook over the fire on a makeshift barbecue of my willow branches. He'd also prepared corn cobs and hominy grits. The first couple of beers died painlessly, and as the sun set shooting mauve streaks across the sky we tore into the food. Night fell quickly and the campfire roared intermittently like a dragon coughing as it was buffeted by gusts of wind. "I always think a nip of Old Jack helps keep the chills out," said John producing a bottle of Jack Daniels from deep within his rucksack and cracking the seal. The catering budget of the Quapaw Canoe Company didn't run to stocking glasses for shorts, so we took turns at nipping from the bottle between us as we talked long into the night. A we talked I found out that there was a lot more to John than met the eye.

"I was born and raised in the Front Range of the Rocky Mountains," John told me, the flames of the blazing campfire lighting him with all the chiaroscuro drama of a portrait by Caravaggio. "In Bear Creek Valley in the shadow of Mount Evans and by the headwaters of the South Fork of the Platte River. I've always been attracted to water, to all expressions of it, whether a pond, a creek, or gutter runoff following a rain storm. They called me the weatherman in school. In first grade my teacher got upset and called my mother one day when I was standing underneath the school roof downspout. It was thunder, lightning, a typical mountain rain storm, but no way was I coming inside." He reached across and picked up the bottle of Jack Daniels from where I had last propped it up in the sand, unscrewed the top and took a drink. He slapped the bottle back into the sand, giving it a twist to anchor it, before he continued. "I first ran away from home when I was two years old. My destination was the duck pond that I could see out of my bedroom window. I like watching the waters ripple in the sparkling Rocky Mountain sunlight. Water has always been calling my name."

As we talked I learnt that John was also a musician, painter and writer. He was the first curator of Clarksdale's Delta Blues Museum and was a co-founder of the Delta Blues Education Fund. But the river always had first claim on John and he founded the Quapaw Canoe Company in 1998, he explained, to provide guided canoe and kayak expeditions on the Lower Mississippi. "It creates one of America's great wildernesses," he said, "a land subject to chaotic weather and the unpredictable character of that Old Man River. It's a landscape of water and sky, broken only by a horizon of willow and mixed deciduous forests. Everything about it is big. Imagine floating a bend of the river that takes 20 miles of delta to complete, or skirting around swirling eddies the size of several city blocks, camping on a sand bar that stretches to the horizon, and swimming in pristine blue holes." I didn't think it was the old Jack that was making John wax lyrical. He was genuinely passionate about the river and the wilderness. "The river had been long neglected, put-down and disrespected. It was lonely and misunderstood. And there was no one on the entire Lower Mississippi, almost a thousand miles of river, who could escort people on her waters and bring them safely back. Many visitors to the South wanted to see the river, to experience it, to touch its currents and learn its ways. Many residents grew up alongside the levee and had never ventured over it to the wilderness on the other side. There was no one to guide them, to show them the way."

I told him that what fascinated me about being out on the river was the whole Huckleberry Finn thing. He smiled. It was obviously a reference he had heard many times before. "I think it goes a lot deeper than that, Bob," he said. "No fossil fuels required. Your arms are the motor in a canoe. Your eyes are the radars. This is as it should be. Americans need reconnecting to the wilderness.

Later, from the open flap of our tent, I watched stabs of sheet lightning light up the sky for miles around until I was too tired to stay awake any longer. My first day on the river had been perhaps more Robinson Crusoe than Huckleberry Finn, not that I was complaining.

I woke to the pitter-patter of rain on the tent. The flap was open and John's sleeping bag lay neatly rolled in a corner. I raised myself onto my elbow and peeked outside. A leaden sky was the colour of dirty pewter. John had somehow managed to revive embers of last night's fire and was crouched over it in a waterproof poncho frying bacon and eggs in a skillet. We ate breakfast in a steady drizzle and then broke camp. Two hours of steady paddling through the wind and rain wasn't much fun but it took us to the town of Helena on the Arkansas side of the river. The sun broke through just as we arrived. One of the great things about arriving in a town in America in a canoe is that you can tie up almost anywhere without having to go in search of a parking lot. We found a grassy stretch of bank right next to the heart of what passed for the downtown, and immediately set about laying out all our wet clothes in the sun to dry. "It should take a couple of hours for the sun to dry 'em," said John, "so go and explore Helena if you want."

The town of Helena, population just over six thousand according to a sign, was a sleepy little place. Even so the community had its own newspaper which punched a little above its weight I thought with the title, The Helena-Arkansas Daily World. I walked around for ten minutes after which I had pretty much explored the neat and tidy confines of Helena. George would have felt right at home here, I thought, it was a Confederate version of Bedford Falls. The only place of any interest that was open was the Delta Cultural Centre. Inside galleries stuffed with display boards and artefacts told the story of Helena, and an interesting tale it turned out to be. Helena may have appeared sleepy and peaceful but its history turned out to be anything but. The first people here, of course, were native Americans who for the best part of 10,000 years had it all to themselves. Next came Spanish and French explorers, and later settlers from all over the US who included European immigrants, searching for a better life. Plantation owners, slaves and dirt poor sharecroppers earned their respective livings, such as they were, from the rich, fertile soil. In the heyday of the Mississippi river boat, Helena was a bustling port and its fortunes had waned with the passing of the stern wheeler.

I was the only visitor so the curator had me all to himself. He was a pleasant, quietly spoken fellow who looked like he had spent his whole life detailing the history of the town. "Where y'all from?" he asked, and when I told him he immediately picked up on my accent and was surprised that someone would come all the way from the UK to visit Helena. "You got family in these parts?" he said. When I told him that John and I were spending a few days canoeing down the river his surprise turned to shocked amazement. "Your museum is preserving a slice of American history," I told him, "well we're actually living a little bit of that history. I've just seen how it was fur trappers in canoes like ours that opened up the American interior". We got talking and he asked me if there was anything I might be particularly interested in, and actually there was.

Years previously I had been transfixed by Ken Burn's historical television documentary series, *The Civil War*. I asked him if Helena had ever featured in the conflict. "Sure," he said, "nearly 2,000 soldiers lost their lives here, most of 'em southerners. Federal forces held the town as it was a key staging post along the Mississippi. The Confederates under General Holmes tried to take it back but the Union forces were well dug in and had set up batteries all around the town. The Battle of Helena took place on July 4th 1863, that date mean anything to you," he asked.

"Independence day," I replied.

"Actually, it's the same day that the Battle of Gettysburg started. We also lost Vicksburg down the river that day to General Grant. You could say that day marked the beginning of the end for the Confederacy, and Helena was involved. Here we lost 1,636 men." His use of the word "we" wasn't lost on me. I had heard talk of southerners who still thought the Civil War, or "the War Between the States" as they preferred to call it in the Deep South. For some southerners it wasn't completely over. I could imagine him at Civil War re-enactments charging at the Union lines screaming the blood curdling Rebel Yell at the top of his lungs. Then getting home, putting on his slippers, donning a pair of half moon glasses and doing a bit of historical research. I was grateful for his personal guided tour but felt that a tip might not be appropriate, so I bought a souvenir plaque of the battle in the gift shop instead. It cost five dollars and I fished into my jeans pocket only to pull out a 50 dollar note. "I'm sorry," I said, "I don't have anything smaller."

"That's okay, sir" he said, taking the note and making change. "There's a picture of Abraham Lincoln on the back of a five dollar bill. "But a fifty," he said with obvious pride as he held up the note, "well, you'll find President Andrew Jackson on the back of a fifty dollar bill, and he was from Tennessee."

Kwissssht! The crackle of static from the short wave radio clipped that was permanently clipped to John's life jacket, startled me. The last two hours had been spent paddling hard against a stiff breeze that blew straight into our faces. It had whisked the mile wide waters into a turbulent froth that rose as high as the sides of the canoe as we pushed against the grip of the river. Coming out of the sweeping bend, one of the many in the Delta that can stretch for miles, the wind shifted behind us. The effect was like throwing a switch. The river calmed in an instant and took on the guise of a vast millpond. We stowed our paddles and I leant back in the canoe and stretched out my aching spine. The sun warmed my face as we let the current take us down. This was exactly the sort of Huckleberry Finn moment I had signed on for I was thinking when the static cleared and a Southern drawl burst from John's chest. "*Heh, looks to me like we gotta couple o' guys out there in a canoe.*" The sound of incredulity in the voice was almost as thick as the accent. Then another voice

replied, "*I see 'em. I tell ya, that sure looks to me like a good way o' gettin'
nowhere fast in a hurry.*"

"Your first tows," said John, pointing over my left shoulder. Pilots on
the river talk to one another constantly, and John always had his radio
tuned in to their frequency so that he could pick up advance warning of
any problems ahead. In the distance two huge lumps appeared to rise
above the surface of the river. They looked like islands, except that islands
don't move, and these two looming shapes were steadily heading straight
for us. "Those are the pilots you can hear talking," said John. "Let's go,"
he said grabbing his paddle and digging in. I did the same and felt the
canoe lift in the water and heard the swish of water rasp under the thin
aluminium hull. But instead of skedaddling out of there, we headed
straight for them. "Man, you're gonna love this," said John.

These industrial, inland waterway leviathans plough their trade up and
down the mid to lower reaches of the Mississippi delivering immense
tonnages of freight. In this respect they are distantly related to the paddle
steamers of Mark Twain's day. But what they lack in style and elegance
they counter with awesome scale. Tow boats don't tow, they push.
And what they push are huge industrial barges which can be loaded with
everything from locomotives to lace tablecloths. A typical barge is sixty
metres long and eleven metres wide, and a single tow can be made up to
forty 40 of these barges lashed together. This creates a slowly moving wall
of rusting metal over 350 metres long and 60 metres wide, covering an
area of over six acres. Mississippi tows are bigger than the average aircraft
carrier, and without doubt are one of the most spectacular sights you can
encounter on the river, especially when seen from the water, up close and
personal, from a small canoe.

The tows are so enormous that they create six feet high waves in their
wakes. We went straight for the first tow's wake, riding the waves rollercoaster style just for the sheer hell of it; the pair of us paddling like mad
things. The trick was to hit each wave head on John told me, otherwise
a wave could capsize us and all the gear. For two exhilarating minutes

we rode wave after wave like a pair of waterborne bucking broncos, John yelling "Yee-ha!" at the top of his lungs as we rode up each wall of water. We would teeter on the crest for a heart-stopping moment, with the canoe more out of the water than in it, and then plunge down the other side, where we only had a few seconds to turn the canoe before the next wave was upon us. John's radio erupted with whoops and whistles from the tows' pilots before one of them saluted us with a long blast of his klaxon that must have been heard halfway across the state.

When John wasn't trying to drown me he proved himself to be a constant mine of information about the river, giving me a running commentary on its flora and fauna as well as pointing out some of its more bizarre aspects. "That's Montezuma Island," he called out as another sandbar island began to slowly slide by for half a mile. "Back in 1829, there was nuthin' here. Then a paddle steamer called the Montezuma burst its boiler and sank right there in the river. What happened was that all the flotsam and trees and vegetation and stuff that floated down, gathered round it and formed this island."

The tows weren't our only source of excitement. Naturally, for a man who was brought up on Mark Twain, John could read the river like a book. To his experienced eye the ever changing patterns of swirling water were like road signs. And some of them spelt danger. Chief amongst these were the underwater dykes that stretched out from the banks and which had been built to control the silting of the river. They caused vicious counter currents. So, too, did the anchored buoys, or "boo-ies", as I often heard the tow pilots call them on John's radio. They created waves and eddies that hissed like angry snakes. Boils were whirlpools, which bubbled up from the depths of the river. Getting caught in one was like sitting on top of a watery mushroom cloud exploding underneath you. "Any of 'em can flip us right over," said John. We spent most of one morning paddling like fury in short sharp bursts as we slalomed in and out of a long line of boils. Then, when the river was kinder, the currents coming off the dykes would gently turn the canoe in complete circles, and we would slowly pirouette down the river in a slow and elegant waltz. This would be John's cue to put down his paddle and pick up his paintbrush and sketchbook. Then he would dip his brush in the river, wipe it over a block of colour and paint in a line of trees with a deft stroke. What would emerge five minutes later would be a stunning watercolour of the Mississippi river, made with real Mississippi river water.

On our last night we bivouacked on another deserted island. Humming birds, no bigger than my thumb, hovered around tall flowers I didn't know the name of, and after the sun went down the air was lit by the flash of fireflies. The tows continued to ply their trade up and down the river and the sweep of their searchlights slashed the darkness like sabres cutting through inky velvet. The silence was broken by the croaking of bullfrogs and the occasional howls of two lonely coyotes, one in the state of Mississippi calling out to its neighbour across the river in Arkansas. Sitting by the fire, finishing off the whiskey, John told me that as well as tourists he also takes local kids with drugs and crime problems on these trips. "There sure ain't nothin' like the river for sortin' a guy out," he said. I believed him. Staring into the roaring fire, and nippin' on the dregs of the Old Jack, I reflected that my most enduring memory would be of a splendid sense of isolation. Earlier in the day we had stopped to drift and let the river take us where it wanted to. Looking up into a sky as big as anything Montana could boast of, I had seen V formations of migrating geese fly by. It was almost impossible to believe that half a mile away on the other side of the levees, lay the world of Taco Bell fast food drive-ins and Piggly Wiggly supermarkets. In the middle of the mile-wide Mississippi you'd never know it. Apart from our stopover in Helena and the voices of the two tow pilots, for the last five days and nights we had been completely cut off from all human contact.

"Finish it off," said John, the bottle made a soft thump as he dropped it into the sand at my feet as he headed for the tent, leaving me to the warmth of the campfire and my thoughts.

The concept of the frontier completely defines the American imagination. It was there in the earliest settler literature. It was present in James Fenimore Cooper's *The Last of the Mohicans* when Hawkeye gazed westwards from present day Ohio towards what must have seemed to him to be a vast unconquerable wilderness. The frontier motivated Lewis and Clark to make their epic journey becoming the first "Americans" to cross the continent. And when Gene Rodenberry penned the lines that opened each episode of Star Trek: *Its continuing mission: to explore strange new worlds, to seek out new life and new civilizations, to boldly go where no one has gone before,* he was echoing Mark Twain's mission to Huck when he sent him down the river with Jim the escaped slave on the run. I felt my week on the river with John had in a very small way actually plugged me into this tradition.

Next morning we broke camp early under a leaden sky. The storm when it came was quick and violent but over within an hour. It cleared the air and we loaded up the canoe for the last time and set off under a cobalt blue sky, the sun making our wet clothes steam as we fell into the now natural rhythm of our paddling. By now I had learnt to enjoy the gentle workout. My muscles had got used to the steady action and it was easy-going with the river doing most of the work. Even so, as we approached our destination, Hurricane Landing, it was good to see the looming figurer of Wesley standing on the bank by the truck.

EIGHT

Alabama Freedom Trail

There's a nondescript street corner in Montgomery, Alabama, where two defining moments in American history took place. On one side of the street, in 1955, a small, black woman named Rosa Parks boarded a public bus. If she had glanced over her shoulder as she stepped on to the bus she would have seen the Winter Building, a rather grand looking antebellum affair where, in 1861, the newly elected president of the Confederate States of America, Jefferson Davis, sent a telegram to his forces in Charleston, South Carolina, ordering them to open fire on the Union garrison at Fort Sumter. It was the action that started the American Civil War. Four years later, slavery in America had been abolished, but nearly a century on, many black Americans living in the Deep South felt that precious little had changed. Reconstruction had merely swapped slavery for segregation. Black Americans drank at segregated public water fountains, ate in their own diners and washed in their own facilities. Another gross indignity was that they sat in their own areas of the buses, or at least they had to in Montgomery.

Who knows what was in her mind as Rosa Parks boarded her bus home that night in 1955 after a long day at the department store where she worked as a seamstress. Like all black Americans she got on at the front, paid the driver her fare, and then had to suffer the indignity of getting off and boarding the bus again at the back. She found one of the last remaining seats and collapsed into it. In the time of travelling a couple of blocks, life in America would never be the same again. At the next stop, more white passengers got on, more than there were seats for, which according to the segregation laws of the time meant that the black passengers had to give up theirs. The bus driver shouted at Parks to give up her seat, but she refused. The police were called and she was arrested. This defiant action, like the Jefferson Davis telegram a century earlier, proved to be the spark that ignited an explosion in American life. The resulting boycott of the Montgomery buses by black Americans lasted over a year. It paved the way for the abolition of segregation in the South; launched the Civil Rights and Voting Rights movements; and catapulted a 26-year-old Baptist minister called Martin Luther King on to the world stage. If my week on the Mississippi with John Ruskey had taught me that the frontier defined the American imagination, then my week in Alabama confirmed that if there's one concept that America holds most dear, it's freedom. But America hasn't always had the most comfortable relationship with this most basic of human rights. Despite the constitution saying, "We hold these truths to be self-evident, that all men are created equal…" social history tells us that since 1776 these words have been subject to wide interpretation, and never more so than when it came to the position of black Americans in society. I learnt this on a guided tour, but it was not like any other guided tour I had ever been on. It told an incredibly moving story: a story that raised heroism to new levels; a story that allowed me to meet some of its heroes at first hand and hear from their own lips what happened; and a story that reached its climax in Montgomery, but started in Birmingham.

I joined a group of 20 or so Americans who would be my companions for the next five days. But what made this tour exceptional was that it wasn't just led by a tour guide in the conventional sense of the word, at every stage we met with people who had taken part in the violent events themselves. Chief amongst them was the Reverend Fred Shuttlesworth who accompanied us throughout the entire five days. The Reverend Fred, as he allowed me to call him, was almost as influential a figure in the Civil Rights Movement as Dr. King. That he has survived well into his dotage was nothing short of a miracle, as I was later to learn. The Rev Fred wasn't tall and was slightly built. But for all that he was imposing with a quiet strength of personality which, one quickly realised, when fully unleashed would have been a force to be reckoned with. He was dapper too, and always appeared wearing a dark blue suit and plain white shirt and tie, which more often than not was topped off, be it a little incongruously, by a white Stetson hat that JR would have been proud to be seen wearing in an episode of the TV show *Dallas*. He spoke in a quiet, deliberate, gravelly drawl. It was a voice that didn't have to raise itself to get listened to.

The Civil Rights Institute in Birmingham told the story of the Civil Rights Movement. It told the story of the struggle of the movement from its earliest days and went back to the days of the Jim Crow laws and beyond. But with the Reverend Fred Shuttlesworth as my guide it was a tour like no other. It was like being shown round Robben Island by Nelson Mandela.

"Education had a big say in the Civil Rights Movement," said Shuttlesworth as he stood beside a display of photographs and newspaper headlines that all talked about Brown versus the Board of Education. He explained that segregation had existed in schools and that this represented a real affront to black Americans, creating a two tier system that kept black children marginalised under a policy of "equal but separate". An early civil liberties organisation the NAACP (National Association for the Advancement of Colored People) argued that this was unconstitutional. On May 17, 1954, the US Supreme Court handed down its decision in favour of the NAACP's lawyers' argument. It was a landmark judgment ending segregation in education. However, it met with strong resistance throughout the Deep South with extreme violence being meted out to black school children and their parents.

The next milestone Shuttlesworth told us about was the Montgomery Bus Boycott, which was inspired by Rosa Parks, "the Mother of the Civil Rights Movement". When she refused to give up her seat on the bus for a white passenger she was immediately arrested and charged with, and later convicted of, disorderly conduct. I had heard of Rosa Parks but had always imagined her to be a quiet, modest woman, and more of a victim than an activist, but Shuttlesworth who knew her told a different story. "At the time she was secretary of the Montgomery branch of the NAACP and had recently attended a convention in Tennessee about non-violent protest," he said. "So the authorities kind of played into our hands." It seems buses were to play an influential role in the life of Rosa Parks. She was raised in dirt poor rural Alabama where white kids were bussed to school but black kids had to walk. As she recalled, "I'd see the bus pass every day. But to me, that was a way of life; we had no choice but to accept what was the custom. The bus was among the first ways I realized there was a black world and a white world"

"When Rosa was arrested the NAACP went into action," said Shuttlesworth, "it was the change they'd been waiting for." They galvanised the black community, largely through its churches, and prompted a bus boycott which lasted 381 days and wrecked the finances of the public bus transport system. Finally, the city authorities repealed its law that allowed segregation following another US Supreme Court ruling that the law was unconstitutional. More importantly, it brought the issue of segregation in the South to the attention of the rest of America and the wider world beyond. It also turned Parks into something of a civil rights celebrity. "Parks's defiance was important for another reason as well," said Shuttlesworth, "the bus boycott in Montgomery brought a previously unknown Baptist minister into the spotlight, Martin Luther King Junior." When Rosa Parks died at the age of 92 Montgomery paid its respects by decreeing that the front seats of the city's buses would be reserved with black ribbons until the date of her funeral. Later her body was laid in state in Washington DC and she was the first woman and only the second black person to be so honoured. Her coffin was carried to her final resting place in a bus similar to the one in which she had made her famous protest.

"The Freedom Rides was something I was more personally involved in," said Shuttlesworth. "I thought it was too dangerous an idea in Alabama where I knew it would be met with levels of violence they'd never seen before, but they were determined to do it anyway, so I went along." The Freedom Rides were bus loads of activists, both black and white, who ignored segregation on buses and in bus terminals. Many of them were northern liberals and this infuriated segregationist southerners, who saw their intervention as none of their business. Chief amongst these groups was the notorious Ku Klux Klan. By then Shuttlesworth knew what he was talking about, as he went on to explain. "The Klan had tried to kill me a few years before," he said, "they blew up my house with 16 sticks of dynamite." He had often been beaten up by Klansman thugs and on one occasion his wife, Ruby, had been stabbed. Shuttlesworth explained that it was the sheer bravery of the Freedom Riders that inspired him to help them. His fears were well founded. When the Freedom Riders arrived in Birmingham, they were violently set upon by Klansmen. Later, an FBI informant said that Birmingham's Public Safety Commissioner, Eugene "Bull" Connor, had done a deal with the Klan giving them a 15 minutes window to attack the Freedom Riders before the police arrived. One white activist was so badly beaten that his head needed 50 stitches. Despite being beaten up himself again earlier in the day, Shuttlesworth took in the Freedom Riders at the Bethel Baptist Church where he was minister, it was just about the only safe place in the city for them. The violence had been so brutal that Bobby Kennedy, who was the Attorney General at the time, gave Shuttlesworth his personal phone number should he need federal support. One of the activists later said of the Reverend Fred Shuttlesworth during the time of the Freedom Rides, "Fred was practically a legend. I think it was important for there to be somebody that really represented strength, and that's certainly what Fred did. He would not back down, and you could count on it."

The Birmingham Campaign of 1963-1964 saw sit-ins at colleges and kneel-ins in churches, and other non-violent protests which were the hallmarks of the Civil Rights Movement. It was at this point that Shuttlesworth led us outside. I hadn't paid much attention to the broad, green garden square when I had arrived at the Institute. The sun was shining, birds sang in the trees that created a patchwork pattern of shade, and people strolled along well tended paths without a care in the world. We crossed over the road into the square and Shuttlesworth said, "We're now standing in Kelly Ingram Park, this is where people really began to take notice." One of the peaceful protests involved hundreds of high school children who congregated outside the 16th Street Baptist Church in defiance of a city ordinance banning mass rallies. Once again, Eugene "Bull" Connor reacted with typical ferocity, and ordered fire hoses and attack dogs to be unleashed on the school children. The violence was captured by TV news cameras and beamed to a shocked and disbelieving world who watched horrified as children were knocked over and sent flying by jets of water, and the jaws of slavering dogs on chains snap at terrified young faces. The American public were outraged by the scenes they witnessed and the Kennedy administration was able to force through some important concessions. But the events at Kelly Ingram Park were to have one more tragic twist in the tale.

The 16th Street Baptist Church stands on the corner of a crossroads overlooking Kelly Ingram Park, hardly any distance at all from the Civil Rights Institute. It's an imposing looking building, stocky and sturdy in red brick with two stumpy towers out front and a wide staircase leading to its front doors, which hover somewhere in between basement and ground floor level. Reverend Shuttlesworth led us over to it but stopped us before we went in. "I used to preach here," he told us, "and so did Dr. King. The 16th Street Baptist Church was a meeting place for many of us in the movement and our supporters, so I guess the Klan saw it as some kind of a symbol." September 15th, 1963, was a Sunday, and a group of 26 young black children were attending the church as part of a special Youth Day. Ironically, they were there to prepare for a sermon entitled The Love That Forgives. As they entered the basement area of the church a bomb made up of 19 sticks of dynamite, which had been planted by four members of the Klan, exploded. Four young girls died in the carnage, and many more children suffered horrendous injuries. A few blocks away, a young girl who was friends with one of the girls that died in the bombing, was performing her piano lessons. "I remember the bombing of that Sunday School at 16th Street Baptist Church in Birmingham in 1963. I did not see it happen, but I heard it happen, and I felt it happen at my father's church. It's a sound that I will never forget, that will forever reverberate in my ears. The bomb took the lives of four young girls, including my playmate, Denise McNair. The crime was calculated to suck the hope out of young lives, bury their aspirations. But those fears were not propelled forward, those terrorists failed." The young piano player was Condoleeza Rice, who years later became America's first black woman Secretary of State.

Inside the church we sat in the wooden pews and listened spellbound as a woman by the name of Carolyn McKinstry recalled how at age 14 she had been one of the school children in the church on that fateful day. Decades later her voice still betrayed the shock and horror of it all as she relived it all moment by moment. Listening to her made me realise that terrorism existed in America long before 9/11. Then we were escorted downstairs into the basement of the church. Long tables had been laid out and in the finest traditions of good old southern hospitality we were served lunch of fried chicken and mashed potatoes, which tasted nothing like anything that ever comes out of a "bargain bucket". Before we sat down to our meal, the Reverend Shuttlesworth was invited to say grace, and then a small, dapper white man in a shirt and tie got up to talk to us. "Hi everyone and welcome," he said before introducing himself, "my name's Doug Jones and I'm the lawyer that put Bob Cherry away, the last of the Klansmen who bombed the church." And with that he set up a projector and for the next half hour gave us an illustrated lecture on how he brought the last remaining bomber to justice. Doug laid out his case one piece of evidence at a time, flashing photos of the exhibits, and photographs of the accused and scenes of the crime on to the projector screen as he spoke. We sat there like members of the original jury taking it all in. It was like having a John Grisham novel read to you out loud, only it was for real. Lunch over, the Reverend Shuttlesworth got to his feet. "Please join me in the hymn of the movement," he said. Everyone stood up and my immediate neighbours left and right grasped my hands. I looked across to see that the whole table had formed a hand-holding human chain as 30 or more voices sang, "We shall overcome..."

Segregation may have been on the wane in the South, but there was another issue that formed a cornerstone of the Civil Rights Movement. Most black Americans in the South were effectively disenfranchised, often through economic as well as physical intimidation and violence. In this way white supremacists were able to remain in power. The Voting Rights Movement grew up around the sleepy little town of Selma. Appropriately, we took a bus to Selma with the Reverend Shuttlesworth sitting at the front. I was seated near the back and noticed that as we left Birmingham a police patrol car fell in behind us and followed us all the way to Selma. Later, I asked the Reverend what that was all about. "The Klan don't give up easily, you know," he said. He was serious too, two state troopers had been sent to accompany us for his protection.

Selma had all the hallmarks of a Deep South town, with wide streets and shady boulevards created by wrought iron arches and balustrades. At the National Voting Rights Museum, we met Joanne Bland, who runs it as a shrine to the ordinary foot soldiers who took part in the protest marches that left from the Brown Chapel in Selma. "Joanne is a veteran of the movement," explained Reverend Shuttlesworth, "she was arrested 13 times." Joanne joined us on the bus and we headed for the Edmund Pettus Bridge, one of the iconic sites of the Civil Rights Movement in Alabama, the scene of what became known as Bloody Sunday. It was a short drive to the bridge and soon as we got going Joanne grabbed the microphone. "In a short while we're gonna be walking over the bridge together," she told us, "so let me tell you about what happened there." Joanne explained that for months leading up to the marches blacks had been targeted by whites as they went to register their right to vote. This culminated one night in a mass, but peaceful, demonstration. When state troopers attacked the demonstrators a young black man, Jimmy Lee Jackson, sought to shelter his mother and grandfather in a cafe, but during the mayhem he was shot by a state trooper. "He died eight days later," said Joanne, "and so the leaders of the Voting Rights Movement decided to organize a mass march from Selma to Montgomery, to attend a special service for Jimmy. A large group of us gathered at the Brown Chapel and then headed for the bridge." The authorities had been forewarned. When Joanne and her fellow marchers arrived at the Edmund Pettus Bridge they were met by an angry mob. Also there were massed ranks of state troopers brandishing billy clubs blocking the road. "Normally," said Joanne, "we would kneel down and pray and then head back to the chapel. I was at the back and suddenly we heard gunshots and screams." What happened next was also caught on camera and beamed across America and around the world. The state troopers boxed in the marchers so they had nowhere to go and systematically set about them with the billy clubs. They also fired tear gas into the crowd. "You couldn't see, you couldn't breathe, all you could do was scream," recalled Joanne, "they were just beating people. If you could outrun the men on foot, you couldn't outrun the ones on horseback. The horses were scared too, they were kicking and rearing up. There was no place for us to go; people were being trampled, being run down by the horses. Blood was everywhere on the bridge and people were laying as if they were dead and we couldn't even stop to see if they were alright, even if you recognised who it was. It was horrible and it seemed to last an eternity." Joanne fainted only to come to in the arms of her sister. She remembers looking up and feeling what she thought were her sister's tears falling on her face.

"But it was blood," said Joanne, "my sister had been clubbed across the head and the wound needed 18 stitches." Joanne was only 11 years old when she went on the first Freedom March and has the distinction of being the youngest ever activist to be arrested.

A short while later we walked across the bridge in the company of Joanne and the Reverend Fred Shuttlesworth. The bridge itself was dominated by a large arch and a span cut through it connecting the two sides of the Alabama river. It wasn't imposing, and neither was it graceful. Two lanes of heavy traffic crossed it in one direction, and two lanes in the other, and there was a pedestrian sidewalk along its edge. Even so, to cross the bridge in such company alongside those who were there, it felt like walking on hallowed ground.

Not long after Bloody Sunday, Dr. King led thousands more on a repeat march that made it all the way to the court house steps at Montgomery. "It was a five-day walk, and on the second day it started raining," Joanne told us, "we slept out in the open and nobody turned around." Once again, the Freedom Marches attracted worldwide media attention, and Congress was quick to act rushing through legislation that guaranteed voting rights.

It only took us an hour to drive the 50 miles to Montgomery from Selma. We travelled in an air-conditioned luxury coach along Highway 80, the very road Joanne Bland and thousands of others had walked along for five days all those years ago. We paid homage at the Dexter Avenue Baptist Church where Dr. King had been minister. By now, it had become apparent to me that the Civil Rights Movement and the Baptist Church in Alabama were inextricably linked. The political system had effectively disenfranchised blacks in the South, so they had no political leaders to turn to. The only community leaders they had to rally round were the Baptist ministers. This gave the movement not only its policy of nonviolence but I suspected also imbued its thousands of participants with a simple faith and an overriding sense of righteousness in their cause. At the Civil Rights Memorial a sheen of water flowed over a black, marble, oval plinth into which had been etched the names of those who had given their lives in the cause – both black and white. Finally, at the Rosa Parks Museum we stood and watched a re-enactment of the famous scene on the bus.

My abiding memory though is of the way everyone responded to the Reverend Fred Shuttlesworth. He may have been a walking, talking, breathing link to one of the darkest chapters in America's history, but wherever we went he was treated like royalty by everyone. I suspect that today's south is a very different place to the one depicted in the Civil Rights story. In Birmingham I had seen both black and white American children wandering the displays in the Civil Rights Institute united in their amazement that life in "mom and pop's" time could have been so different. Watching them made me think if anywhere should be franchised and set up in every school in the USA it was the Civil Rights Institute.

NINE

The Real Bedford Falls

I had been to New York before, be it very briefly. It had been a business trip. I'd been sent over with Rupert Murdoch's international marketing guru to do some work on a TV listings magazine that had just been added to the Murdoch empire. Graham King was a grizzled looking, wily, no nonsense Aussie who also happened to be a marketing and promotions genius. More than that he was simply a great bloke who was very supportive of creative people like me, and he could down Chardonnay in the way I shifted pints. We had spent a couple of weeks at the magazine's headquarters which were based in Radnor, a completely forgettable town about an hour's drive from Philadelphia. At the end of the trip, Graham had been summoned to a meeting with Murdoch in New York, and as a reward for my efforts in Radnor he took me with him. It was a flying visit, literally we were there for only 24 hours, except that unlike most first time visitors to New York from the UK I didn't fly in, but arrived via Amtrak train. The problem with flying into New York, for the first time visitor anyway, is that you see the city in long shot well before you get there, which kind of dampens the effect. The train from Philadelphia disappeared into a tunnel before I caught a sight of the city, so when I emerged from Grand Central station, Kapow! There it was, New York City towering up above me. What made it even better was it was ten o'clock at night and New York wasn't just towering but blazing with lights. We checked into our hotel and within minutes were back on the streets and looking for a bar. Graham was determined that my first drink in Manhattan should be a Manhattan.

The next morning Graham disappeared for his pow wow with Rupert and I had a day to myself in the most exciting city in the world. The first thing I did was catch a subway train down to the World Trade Centre. The Twin Towers were an awesome sight in the crisp, cool, clear early morning light. I walked across to the foot of one of the towers, I couldn't tell you if it was the North or South tower, and stood and looked up. Then I stretched out my hand so I was actually touching the tower, and even thought I was physically in contact with what I was looking at, I still couldn't believe what I was seeing. In many ways this will always sum up for me the entire New York experience.

To be honest, there was one other incident that also made New York stick in the mind, and it was straight out of Damon Runyan. Ever since I had first seen *Guys and Dolls* I had always wanted to visit Times Square and follow in the footsteps of Nathan Detroit, Sky Masterson, Little Isidore and all the other characters, who through their wit and guile, scammed their various ways through life. So as the great chronicler himself of life on the lam in New York in the roaring twenties might have told it… It is four o'clock in the morning and I am leaving a cosy little speak on Broadway and ruminating on this very subject when a cab draws up and out steps a very elegant looking doll onto the sidewalk. The doll takes one look at me and says, "Would you like some company honey?" Now this is most unusual as good-looking dolls rarely approach me in this way, and before I can make with an answer she says, "What hotel you stayin' in?" I explain to the doll that I am staying at a very exclusive establishment off Central Park West, but that I am sharing a suite with a very important business travelling companion who would not take it kindly by being disturbed by the presence of a good-looking doll, especially when he has an early meeting the next morning with the world's most powerful media baron. I am also thinking that this will make me a non-runner in her eyes, thus allowing me to ditch the doll in a courteous and polite manner, my having been brought up to always being courteous and polite when dealing with dolls.

"That's goin' my way," says the doll, "mind if I tag along." As we walk north up Broadway there is more general chit-chat along what most dolls are good at making, and by the time we have walked a couple of blocks, she knows most about what I am doing in the city. "Look," she says, "Why don't you give me call next time you're in New York?"

"Good idea," I say, because that's precisely what it is, it gets me out of a jam with a neat exit. So the doll stops, takes my arm and we step into a doorway. She is digging around in her handbag and produces a notebook and pencil. But instead of writing down her John Doe and phone number she hands them to me to do the business with. "So, what's your name?" I ask her. "Euphemia," she replies. Now Euphemia is a pretty uncommon name for a doll in anyone's language, and not expecting her to part with her real monicker anyway, I play right along and ask her to spell it out for me, which she does. So while I have my hands full and the doll is spelling out her name, she gives me the clincher. I use the word literally because, uninvited, she takes hold of me in a place that last time I was grabbed down there, I was 12 years old and the doctor was asking me to cough. "You absolutely sure, honey?" the doll purrs. I decline and escape into the night to wave down a cab. Minutes later the cab drops me off outside my hotel. I reach into my trouser pocket to pay the fare and guess what – no spondoolicks. In fact, no scratch left whatsoever. The doll lifts over 200 hundred dollars, and she does it with no black-jack-wielding accomplice, no mace spray; just a lot of skill and no little dexterity. A bang up job by a very clever doll. So I had to wake up the poor sap anyway to loan me wedge to pay the cab driver.

George never even made it to big bad New York City even though Bedford Falls was in New York State. The most exciting, vibrant, multi-cultural city on the planet and it was only down the road. Practically everyone else who lived in Bedford Falls went there at one time or another. George's old friend Sam Wainwright went and made a fortune in plastics. George's brother went there. Even Mary went to college there, but not "old moss-back George" as Sam Wainwright used to call him. How cruel was that? Especially as George spent his life in the house building trade. Even if it was only social housing, George would have been blown away by the scale and variety of the architecture of New York. Once again, I would only tally 24 hours in New York. I was booked out on a flight to Albany the next morning, although I hoped to fit in a few days on my return before flying back to the UK. But journeys end was beckoning, Seneca Falls, the town that called itself the real Bedford Falls, was hosting its *It's A Wonderful Life* festival, and having been round the world and "done it" for George I was excited about finishing off my odyssey by immersing myself in the life of the world's favourite feel-good movie.

With a name like Denise Champagne, she should have been editing a glossy fashion magazine from a high-rise corner office overlooking Fifth Avenue. Instead, Denise was sitting in a poky little office next to Sammy's barber shop, where she worked as the Seneca Falls reporter for the Finger Lakes Times. There's a scene early in the love story part of the movie when Mary Hatch returns from having spent a few years away at college in New York City. George can't believe that anyone who got away would want to possibly come back, so he asks why she's returned and she tells him she felt homesick. Actually, it's because she's secretly in love with George and has been since she was a little girl, but she's not telling him. "Homesick," says George incredulously, "for Bedford Falls". He makes it sound like missing toothache. Well, Denise sounded much the same when I told her why I was here. "You've come all the way from England? To write about the town?"

"Yes," I said, "It's A Wonderful Life is my favourite movie and I heard that Seneca Falls claims to be the real Bedford Falls."

"Jeez," said Denise, grabbing the phone, "you better talk to Fran Caraccilo. This whole Bedford Falls thing was his idea."

Seneca Falls lies in the middle of the Finger Lakes region of New York State, about four hours drive from New York City, and only a couple of hours drive from the Canadian border. I hired a car at Albany airport and drove into Seneca Falls to see the town decked out for the Christmas holidays, and with Andy Williams singing *It's The Most Wonderful Time of the Year* popping up almost every quarter hour on the car radio. First impressions were a bit of a shock because the town was in colour, the movie version, of course, being seared into my memory in black and white.

I met Fran Caraccilo in the appropriately named Zuzu's cafe on Fall Street. Zuzu was George and Mary's youngest child in the film, who George called his little ginger snap. She was played by a six year old Karolyn Grimes, who was guest of honour in Seneca Falls for the festival. In fact, she was sitting three tables away signing autographs. "I grew up loving the film," Fran told me, "and I was convinced that there were similarities between Seneca Falls and the Bedford Falls that Capra depicted in the movie." Fran had worked for years as the town planner he told me, so he knew the town inside out. "Me and my wife would watch the film whenever it came on TV and each time we'd spot a new similarity between Seneca Falls and the fictional Bedford Falls on screen. That's what got me started." Fran started digging and the more he dug the more convinced he was that Seneca Falls was the inspiration for Bedford Falls. Fran then proceeded to lay out his evidence like a lawyer. "The characters in the film make references throughout to nearby towns: Elmira, Rochester and Buffalo," he said, "and the main street here used to have a grassy strip running down the middle of it, just like the main street in the movie when George runs down at the end shouting Merry Christmas Bedford Falls. We also know that Frank Capra visited here when the movie was still in the script planning stages," he said idly stirring his coffee, "we've got Tommy Bellisima to thank for that." Tommy Bellisima, Fran explained had a barber shop in Seneca Falls in 1945. Capra was passing through Seneca Falls on his way to visit his aunt who lived in nearby Auburn and he stopped off on the way at Tommy's to get a haircut. "Tommy didn't realise it at the time but the man sitting in his barber's chair was the famous Hollywood director," said Fran, "but when the movie came out he recognised the name in the credits on the screen. The two men were both of Italian immigrant stock and had talked about their families' experiences, and Tommy remembered the name Capra because in Italian it means goat. But heh, maybe I'm getting a little bit ahead of myself here, how well do you remember the movie?"

"Pretty good," I said, "but I'm sure you recall it better."

"I like to walk people up to the Truss Bridge near the site of Tommy's shop. We can go up there if you like, and what I usually do is give people a potted version on the way."

So leaving Karolyn Grimes to her line of adoring fans who snaked around two of the walls of the cafe waiting in line to get her autograph, we ducked out into the cold. The sky was dark overhead with the threat of fresh snow and frosted slush crunched under our boots as we made our way up Fall Street.

"The movie began as a short story," Fran said as we headed off along Main Street. "A guy called Philip Van Doren Stern had an idea for a short story which he wrote up and called *The Greatest Gift*. He sent it around a few publishers but nobody was interested, so he got it made up as a pamphlet and sent it out as a Christmas card to his family and friends. One of them ended up in Hollywood and a few months later he got Western Union telegram offering him 10,000 dollars for it." Fran explained that then as now, once Hollywood gets its claws into a literary property the writer can expect the story to change radically. And so it proved with the script of *It's A Wonderful Life*. Fran didn't know how Mr. Van Doren Stern had felt about that, but I reckoned that back in the 1940s ten grand sounded like a pretty good pay out. Then Fran proceeded to give me his potted version of the story as it was told in the movie.

It's Christmas Eve and George Bailey (James Stewart) is contemplating suicide. Family and friends pray for him. In heaven an angel second class, Clarence Odbody (Henry Travers) is summoned and told that George is about to throw away God's greatest gift, and is then charged to go down and save George from himself. If he's successful, Clarence is told, he'll earn his wings and become a fully fledged angel. But before Clarence is dispatched earthwards he's given a rundown on George Bailey's life and what has brought him to this terrible juncture. We see George at the age of 12 playing with a group of kids on a frozen pond. One of them, George's younger brother Harry, falls through the ice and George dives in and rescues him, losing the hearing in one ear as a result. George grows up with dreams of travelling the world but circumstances and responsibilities always conspire to keep him home. The family runs the Bailey Building and Loan, a much needed socially minded financial institution that helps poor working class people be able to afford their own modest homes. The alternative for them is to live in one of the slum dwellings run by the town's richest and meanest man, Mr. Potter (Lionel Barrymore). George waits for his brother Harry to come back from college to take over the running of the firm, but when Harry arrives back in Bedford Falls he turns up with a wife in tow and a job offer from his new father-in-law. George does the decent thing and gives up on his dreams of travelling the world. Next he calls on Mary Hatch (Donna Reed) who is fresh back from college. Mary has held a candle for George since she was a little girl, and once whispered "I'll love you George Bailey till the day I die," in his deaf ear. They get married and are about to go on honeymoon when there is a run on the bank that threatens to kill off the Bailey Building and Loan. Mary gives George their honeymoon money to rescue the firm and they set up home in the run down old Granville House, where they raise four kids. When World War Two breaks out George can't enlist and stays home because of his deaf ear. Meanwhile, brother Harry becomes a pilot and a hero when he shoots down 15 enemy planes, two of which were about to sink a troop carrier carrying thousands of troops. All this is told in flashback and then we return to the morning of the fateful Christmas Eve. George's absent-minded Uncle Billy is on his way to the bank to deposit $8,000 when he runs into Mr. Potter who hates the Bailey family. Uncle Billy has a copy of the newspaper splashed with the headline about Harry being awarded the Medal of Honor, and taunts Mr. Potter with it. Potter angrily grabs the newspaper in which Uncle Billy has absentmindedly placed the $8,000 cash. Later, Potter realises Uncle Billy's mistake and decides to keep the cash knowing full well that with the money unaccounted for, George, as head of the Bailey Building and Loan, will face bankruptcy and disgrace. And the bank examiner is due that very day to audit the books. When a distraught Uncle Billy confesses to George that he's somehow lost the money, George goes crazy. He knows he's facing ruin and prison. In desperation George goes to Potter, who is the only man with that kind of money in town, and pleads with him to give him a loan. The only collateral George can offer Potter is a paltry life insurance policy worth 500 dollars. Potter turns George down flat, saying to George, "Why, you're worth more dead than alive". George goes home and fights with Mary and the children who are decorating the family Christmas tree. Then he storms out of the house and goes to Martini's Bar and gets blind drunk. After a few more drinks, and with the words of Potter echoing in his ears – "You're worth more dead than alive" – George staggers to the Truss Bridge over the canal. He is about to end it all and throw himself into the dark, cold, swirling waters when Clarence the angel appears. Clarence has a brainwave and throws himself into the water pretending to commit suicide. The sight of a drowning man shocks George back into reality and he dives in to save Clarence. Clever old Clarence knew George would do this so by pretending to end his own life Clarence saves George's life instead. While they're drying off in a lock keeper's cottage, Clarence explains to George that he's an angel and has been sent down to help George in his hour of need. George naturally doesn't believe him and tells Clarence he wishes he'd never been born. This gives Clarence another idea and he grants George his wish, telling George, "Okay, you've never been born". The pair of them head back into Bedford Falls only to discover that the town and everyone in it has changed beyond all recognition. What was a caring community has turned into a nightmare of greed and sleaze. The good people of Bedford Falls, George's friends and neighbours, are all bitter and twisted. George staggers from one encounter to another, with a patient Clarence in tow, and learns that because he had never been born the lives of everyone around him have totally changed. His brother Harry died falling through the ice when they were kids because George wasn't around to save him. The hundreds of soldiers on the troop ship all died because Harry wasn't there to save them either. Uncle Billy is in an asylum for the insane, and George's mother is a venal old woman who runs a shady boarding house. Finally, George tracks down Mary only to discover that she never married and is a dried-up, spinster living a lonely life as a librarian. Seeing all this George begs Clarence to give him his life back. His plea is answered and he runs home to Mary and the kids where the police, who have been tipped off by Potter, are waiting to arrest him. But just as they are about to snap the cuffs on George, the good people of the town arrive in their hordes with their savings in cash to bail him out. Even George's brother, Harry, flies in from Washington and proposes a toast to, "My big brother George, the richest man in town". George, surrounded by his adoring Mary, his loving children, and all his friends and neighbours, realises the essential message of the film: that no man who has friends is a failure and that life really is a precious gift. As for Clarence, he gets promoted to angel first class.

Fran drew to the end of his summing up just as we got to the Truss Bridge. "Tommy's barber shop was just over there," he said, pointing towards a street corner opposite. "When Capra left after getting his hair cut he would have had to cross the bridge to get back into town. Now, come and take a look at this." The bridge looked just like the one from the film. The grey, ironwork structure was fringed with snow and billowy flakes began to fall and swirl as the wind picked up. It was cold, it was bleak, it was wintry, and for someone contemplating suicide, it was perfect. Frank led me over to a commemorative plaque that was bolted to the iron structure at one end of the bridge. It was dedicated to a young man, Antonio Varacalli, who in 1917 had been crossing the bridge on just such a wintery night when he saw a suicidal young woman jump from the bridge into the water below. He jumped after her and grabbed hold of her. Then he fought the swirling water and the madly thrashing young woman and managed to drag her close enough to the bank for another passer-by to haul her out of the water. But, overcome by the cold and exhaustion, Antonio Varacalli was powerless to fight the grip of the icy current and was swept away and drowned. "It's exactly the plot from the movie when Clarence saves George by jumping into the canal," said Fran, "and Capra would have seen this plaque." Fran delivered this final, irrefutable piece of evidence with all the flamboyance of a grand-standing barrister declaring to the members of the jury that the case for the defence rests. I had to admit, he had made a very convincing argument.

In the film George and Mary lived in the Granville House, a big, sprawling Victorian affair with a touch of the Gothic about it. The house first appears in the film when George, having danced with Mary at the school prom and famously fallen into the underfloor swimming pool, walks her home past the old house. Mary stops and looks across the street at the deserted, ramshackle, pile and tells George how she's always loved the place. George tells her that the story goes that if you pick up a rock, make a wish and throw the rock and break one of the old house's windows, then your wish will come true. So George picks up a rock and hurls it at the house and we hear the sound of breaking glass. Mary asks George what he wished for and he tells her: "Oh, not just one wish. A whole hatful. Mary, I know what I'm going to do tomorrow, and the next day, and next year, and the year after that. I'm shakin' the dust of this crummy little town off my feet and I'm gonna see the world. Italy, Greece, the Parthenon, the Coliseum. Then, I'm comin' back here to go to college and see what they know. And then I'm gonna build things. I'm gonna build airfields. I'm gonna build skyscrapers a hundred stories high. I'm gonna build bridges a mile long ..." Mary bends down and picks up a rock of her own, throws it, and once again we hear the sound of breaking glass. "Hey, that's pretty good," says George, "What'd you wish for Mary?" But George's question isn't answered until much later in the film when Mary turns the old Granville House into the new Bailey family home. Seneca Falls had more of its fair share of such domestic architecture, and a few of them had been turned into guesthouses. I picked the one I thought most resembled the house in the film.

Barristers was a charming B&B run by Judy. A log fire spat and crackled in the grate and highly polished mahogany bookcases, tables and plushly upholstered furniture reflected the firelight, casting warm, amber reflections across the wood parquet floor. George and Mary's house never attained such heights of luxury. Far from it, George was forever complaining about the draughty old place and every time he walked upstairs the knob at the end of the banisters came off in his hand. To be honest I was a bit disappointed that the same thing didn't happen to me and thought about suggesting to Judy that she should chisel hers loose. But casting my eye around the meticulously maintained house told me that such an idea would never have figured in Judy's thinking, especially as she catered for a far more discerning clientele than I represented. "We get New Yorkers coming for the weekend," Judy told me, "and Karolyn Grimes stayed with us the first time she came here for the festival." Next morning I decided to go and explore the rest of Seneca Falls and see if the spirit of the movie could also be found in the community at large. The early portents proved favourable, Judy served me up a rib-sticking breakfast of porridge with fresh blueberries. Even the food in Seneca Falls was good and wholesome. "You're famous," said Judy as she collected my bowl and poured coffee, dropping a copy of the newspaper on the table, and there grimacing back at me was my photograph on the front page of the Finger Lakes Times. While I had been up at the Truss Bridge with Fran yesterday Denise Champagne had been busy. The fact that a travel writer had come all the way from England to write about the town was news in Seneca Falls apparently, even if I had taken a somewhat circuitous route in getting here which Denise had deliberately failed to mention.

Consequently, when I hit the street and strolled the five minutes into town I was greeted by a battery of good natured waves, beaming smiles, "Good mornings" and "Merry Christmases" from everyone I passed on the street. If I needed any further proof that I was something of a celebrity in small town America I didn't have to wait long. As I approached Fall Street a charming couple in their sixties stopped me and enquired after my health and asked how I was enjoying visiting the town. I assured them I was having a high old time, whereupon the woman said, "And we hope you enjoyed your meatloaf at Connie's Diner last night." People on the street knew what I'd eaten. A number of the shops and offices I walked past all had the word community in their title. I made my way to the Centre for the Voices of Humanity where Karolyn Grimes was bestowing the George Bailey Award for the citizen of the year. The worthy recipient this year was Bob Branciforte, the barber at Sammy's barber shop, which was located right next door to Denise Champagne's office. In fact, they shared the same porch. Bob had smiled at me when her photographer had taken me outside to take the photo that ended up in the paper. Perhaps Bob had thought that I had needed a hair cut to smarten up my appearance before it was syndicated throughout the Finger Lakes region. I was late and the room was packed when I got there. From the back, looking over people's heads, I could see a very happy looking Bob holding his award and having his photograph taken next to a smiling Karolyn Grimes. I had missed the citation so had no idea how long Bob's list of good deeds over the last 12 months ran to. I thought it safe to assume that his contribution to the community went further than not fleecing his neighbours when they came in for a short back and sides. Being voted best citizen in this town was probably more akin to a full time occupation rather than a bit of volunteering at weekends.

In the part of the film where Bedford Falls and its people change out of all recognition, George takes Clarence to Martini's Bar where Nick, the barman, tells him: "Hey, look mister, we serve hard drinks in here for men who want to get drunk fast." So, did Seneca Falls also have a darker side, I wondered? That night I found out. Outside Dewey's 3rd Ward Tavern, pick-up trucks with gun-racks in their rear windows lined the car park. Inside the roadhouse bar men sat on tall bar stools, necking Buds by the bottle staring at the banks of TV screens fixed to the walls showing NFL Football, NBA Basketball and ice hockey games from Canada. Women in leather jackets and tight jeans shimmied to a Kenny Rogers track playing on the juke box. Suddenly, I had left the world of Frank Capra and walked into a scene from a David Lynch movie. Or so I thought, until a tall, attractive woman who was shooting pool sashayed over to me and said, "Hi, I'm Diana, I'm the mayor and I've heard all about you. If there's anything you need while you're in town, you give my office a call." And with that she handed me her business card and invited me to shoot a few frames with her. "You rack 'em up Bob and I'll go get us both a couple of beers." In Seneca Falls, even the dives are respectable.

Karolyn Grimes was six years old when she played Zuzu, the youngest of the Bailey children in the film. Over 60 years later she stood at a lectern by a projector screen in the Seneca Falls Community Centre. The lights went down and a black and white moving image flickered into life on the screen. There was an audible gasp from the audience as James Stewart dashed into his youngest daughter's bedroom where Zuzu is sitting up in bed holding her broken flower. Judging by her thick, shoulder-length blonde hair, attractive smile and neat figure, the passing years had been kind to Karolyn Grimes. Later, I learnt her life had not been so wonderful. Behind her, framed in the floor-to-ceiling windows stood the brooding presence of the Truss Bridge over the Seneca Falls Canal. For the next half hour Karolyn showed us clips from the film and recalled her childhood memories of making the movie. "Of course, the movie was shot on a huge, specially constructed set in Hollywood," she said, "and I was fascinated by the fake snow because I had never seen snow before." The audience was made up of local people, people from out of town out of town, It's A Wonderful Lifers, and film buffs who had travelled miles to be here and hear Karolyn speak. They hung on her every word. For most of them Christmas simply wasn't Christmas without watching the movie, and the singing of *Buffalo Girls Won't You Come Out Tonight*, George and Mary's courting song, was as much a Christmas carol as *Hark The Herald Angels Sing*.

After her talk we stayed around and mingled and swapped *It's A Wonderful Life* trivia. I learnt that it was Jimmy Stewart's favourite film out of all the ones he made, and that Frank Capra was known as the poet of the common man. One of the anomalies of the film is that Mr. Potter never gets his comeuppance for stealing away the $8,000, and I was told that Capra shot a scene where Mr. Potter is confronted by Clarence with the knowledge of his crime but that Capra never used it in the final cut. Before the evening ended I was able to grab a few minutes with Karolyn Grimes. "Will you be watching the film at home with your family over the holidays?" I asked. "No," she replied looking a little embarrassed. "I didn't bring my kids up on the film because I didn't want to be a show-off mom."

"And where is home?" I asked her.

"Kansas," she replied. It seemed that Zuzu had in real life turned into something of a Dorothy, but in talking to her it quickly became clear that her life had not been an over-the-rainbow happy one. Her mother died when she was 14, and then her father died a year later in a car crash. She was fostered out to her aunt and uncle who worked a farm in Missouri. It was not a happy time. "Hollywood quickly became a distant memory. I got married, raised kids and worked as a medical technician," she told me. But she lost her husband in a hunting accident, a son committed suicide and when she remarried her second husband later died of cancer leaving her with seven children to raise. If anyone from the film had had their faith well and truly tested, I thought, it had to be Karolyn Grimes, and she came across as a brave and positive woman. She certainly possessed an easy charm and had time for everyone who approached her, and when she said on umpteen occasions that she still believed in the message of the film, she knew it was important for people to hear her say that, and she never disappointed anyone. "It's all about how each of us touches so many other peoples' lives. It's about how each one of us makes a difference. And it gives us inspiration because it makes us think about what's important in our lives," she said to people many times that evening. But she was game for a laugh too. When I told her I wanted my photograph taken with her I asked her if we could repeat the famous pose from the movie poster, with Zuzu riding piggy back on James Stewart with her arms round his neck. She shot me a funny look saying, "Heh, I'm not as young as I used to be."

"Don't worry, I'll crunch down," I reassured her. And a trooper to the end, she wrapped her arms around me and we got the shot. Seems like you can take the girl out of Hollywood but despite all her travails you couldn't completely take Hollywood out of Karolyn Grimes. I was aware that becoming an ambassador for the film, and regularly attending the Seneca Falls festival, had obviously given Karolyn a new lease of life and a much needed boost financially. So it was with a hint of cynicism that I asked her, "So Karolyn, do you really think this is the real Bedford Falls?"

"You know what," she said, "I was sceptical at first, but when I laid my eyes on this place I knew right away, this is Bedford Falls."

Maybe she was still a very convincing actress even after all these years, or maybe she wanted to believe it so much she had convinced herself, or maybe in her heart of hearts she was genuinely totally convinced. Who could say, and anyway it was Christmas. All I know is that Capra's opening shot of *It's A Wonderful Life* is of a snow-encrusted street sign that reads: You are now in Bedford Falls. Having visited Seneca Falls and met the real Zuzu, the next day I left convinced that I had been there.

Postscript

Back In New York I had a day to kill before I flew home. The last day of my round the world adventure saw me visit a place where so many other people's new world one had started, Ellis Island. I took the ferry from the Battery on the southern tip of Manhattan Island. We passed the Statue of Liberty – *Give me your tired, your poor, your huddled masses yearning to breathe free. The wretched refuse of your teeming shore. Send these the homeless, tempest tossed to me: I lift my lamp beside the golden door.* And Europe did. That great tidal wave of humanity that washed across the entire United States between 1892 and 1954 was funnelled through Ellis Island. In a period of just over 60 years, over 12 million immigrants made the journey in the hope of a better life. As the ferry dropped us off at Ellis Island I felt in a very small way a strange affinity with them. I would be returning home in the opposite direction tomorrow. And perhaps like all those immigrants to the prospect of a new way of life, too.

Ellis Island ceased being the immigration centre that processed people into the United States in 1954 and it had been mothballed for many years. In 1990 it was reopened as a national monument and museum of immigration. The fabric of the building had been beautifully preserved both inside and out. A walking tour has been designed so that you went through Ellis Island very much in the footsteps of the 12 million immigrants who preceded you.

The vast majority of immigrants who landed at Ellis Island were accepted into the United States straight away, but nearly a million were sent back, the majority of them failing to gain entry on health grounds. As they assembled in the Great Hall, and were subjected to health checks by the medical orderlies, they could clearly see across the water the skyline of Lower Manhattan. The sense of being so near, yet so far must have been unbearable. The anxiety was etched into the faces of those immigrants that stared out from the sepia print photographs that lined the walls.

One of them in particular caught my eye. It had been blown up to poster size and was captioned: *Italian Child, Ellis Island, 1926. This little girl finds the wonders of Ellis Island and the New World more fascinating than the first penny clasped in her hand.* She looked no more than six years old, Karolyn Grimes's age when she played Zuzu. So there was a good chance that if she had been one of the hardier ones she might still be alive. It was a compelling image and made me wonder what might have come of her. Did she grow up to marry a nice Italian boy from the same village back home? Being of peasant stock perhaps her family headed west to settle on the prairie lands, or did she grow up to be sucked into the burgeoning industrialisation of the big cities? Did she end up working behind a shop counter or in a schoolroom? Did her children grow to become policemen or gangsters, businessmen or politicians, Pennsylvania coalminers or Pittsburgh steelworkers? Did she forever speak English with her native Calabrian accent? Perhaps she still lived somewhere in New York and could see Ellis Island from her window. Or perhaps she and her family moved to Chicago, or Cleveland, or Detroit, or Phoenix, or Philadelphia, or San Francisco, or Des Moines, Iowa, and started a new life there. Who knows, she might even have settled in New York State in a small town like Bedford Falls. Her father might even have opened a bar there like Martini's in the film. It seemed like the entire immigrant experience had been captured in all its hopes and fears in one hastily taken snapshot. And there had been millions and millions of others just like her: young and old, Jewish and Christian, Slav and Basque, Pole and Irish, German and Greek, Russian and Romany. It was hard to believe that those waifs and lost souls, many of them carrying their one change of clothes in a brown paper parcel tied up with string, would quickly become the living, breathing raw material that fuelled the economic explosion that in a relatively few short years catapulted the United States of America into the first rank. I hoped that she had made out all right. I wanted her to have been one of the lucky ones, to have lived the American Dream, not a nightmare.

As I left I picked up a leaflet and idly stuffed it in my pocket. A couple of hours later I was in a cab to take me to JFK and my flight home. It was dark and the skyscrapers of Midtown Manhattan were ablaze with lights. It was then that I remembered the leaflet and took it out of my pocket. As I flicked through it a name I recognised suddenly jumped out at me. Under the heading: Some Were Destined For Fame was a list of the immigrants who had passed through Ellis Island and gone on to realise their own American Dreams, and there he was, third name down on the list: *Frank Capra, Film Director, who came through Ellis Island from his native Italy in 1903 when he was six years old.* You couldn't script an ending like that, I thought, not even in Hollywood.